THE RHODE ISLAND DICTIONARY

SPOCK PLUG

MARK PATINKIN

Illustrated by DON BOUSQUET

Covered Bridge Press
7 Adamsdale Road
N. Attleboro, MA 02760

(508) 761-5414

A FEW WORDS OF THANKS

First, I'd like to thank Don Bousquet, master of Rhode Island cartoon humor. This project was his idea. I might never have done it had he not called after reading a column I did on Rhode Islandese and suggested we join together to make a book of it. I remain indebted to him for bringing these pages alive with the kind of illustrations we've all come to know as his unique style and gift.

At first, I didn't think it would be a difficult project, but it grew and grew, chewing up many more months than I expected, so my next thanks goes to my wife Heidi and two young children. I hope they forgive me for all the lost weekends, evenings and early mornings; and looking back, I don't blame my 2-year-old for the times he came into my study and tried to get my attention by pushing the ''delete'' button on my computer. He succeeded. And I have a special debt to my wife for her proof-reading, suggestions and guidance. Whatever flaws this book may have, it has fewer because of her.

I'd also like to thank Chuck Durang and Doug Paton, the principals of Covered Bridge Press, my publisher. They kept faith with me as I missed deadline after deadline. But somehow, despite my own lateness, they managed to get this book out on schedule. For that efficiency, and especially, for their belief in this project, I'll forever be grateful.

I'm grateful as well to my editors at the Providence Journal: Jim Wyman, Joel Rawson, Carol Young and Andy Burkhardt. They give me freedom most journalists - in fact, most workers - only hope for, and I'll always feel indebted to them for that.

And a final thanks goes to my invaluable associates in the writing of this project: the hundreds of people who sent in letters bearing suggestions. Many of their ideas have found their way into these pages. I wish I had the space to print all their names. And though a journalism teacher once warned me to never lean on old cliches in writing, I can't think of a better phrase than this for those letter writers: I couldn't have done this without you.

THE STORY BEHIND THIS BOOK

I decided to write this dictionary as a celebration of one part of Rhode Island's uniqueness. It's a book about how we talk: we tend to do it differently than anywhere else. It's also a book of humor - attempted humor anyway - which fits in with another part of Rhode Island I find worth celebrating: our ability to laugh at ourselves.

A few months before I began this project, I wrote three newspaper columns for the Providence Journal-Bulletin on what might be called Rhode Islandese. I gave examples of how we tend to leave out the letter 'r' where it's supposed to be - bubbla and cah - and add it where it's not supposed to be - soder and lawr. By rough estimate, I got several hundred letters suggesting other examples of Rhode Islandese. I don't think I've gotten that much mail on any subject since I criticized cats. In this case, all but about four or five of the letters joined in the humor. Okay, maybe a half dozen.

What did the half dozen negative letters have to say? Well, those readers felt that chronicling the way Rhode Islanders' speak sounded like mocking. One such letter writer offered her own story of Rhode Islandese concerning the time in K-Mart she heard a nearby shopper debating whether to buy a pair of "fidallah" shoes, and found herself wondering if "fidallah" was a fancy word for the color of the shoes, which were an odd shade of peacock blue. But that same reader then wondered whether this whole business of writing about dialect might be belittling.

To her, and all others out there who feel that way, I'd like to say two things. First, I respect anyone who loves this state enough to defend it so sincerely. But second, those columns - and this book - have been written by someone proud to call Rhode Island home, and fond of our distinctiveness. My goal is not to mock the accent, but to capture it, and have fun doing so. I was amused to see that I got scores of letters from places like Johnston and Cranston - which some might call two epicenters of the Rhode Island accent - showing perhaps the best sense of humor on the issue of all. Don't forget the Rhode Island vowel, one reader from Cranston said, and then spelled it out: "Ayyyy." And several from Johnston wanted to make sure I added to any future columns what they called the Rhode Island greeting: "Yo." As in, "Yo, Vinnie."

Even priests joined in. One suggested the words "Yessta" and "Nosta." Translation: "Yes sister," and "No sister," - principally heard around Catholic schools. And a reader named Connie Worthington sent me a xerox of a page from the Providence phone book. She circled the point where the last name "Larson" begins. There are about a dozen of them in the book, and right beforehand, the helpful folks at NYNEX added this tip: "See also Lawson." Which means even the phone company has officially acknowledged our accent. As a true Rhode Islander might say, izzat great, awwutt?

So our language is indeed distinctive, but Rhode Island hasn't gotten nearly the attention for it as other places have gotten for their own dialects. The most noted, of course, is the Southern accent. We've even had a couple of Presidents, including the current one, who speak it. Plenty of people have had fun trying to capture it, pointing out such words as 'arn', 'tar', 'yale' and 'speer.' Which are Southern for iron, tire, yell and superior.

Then, a few years back, a lot of attention was given to a newly discovered California dialect called 'Valley-Speak.' Suburban Los Angeles teenaged girls were the tribe most notably associated with it. They used phrases like, 'Gag me with a spoon', 'Ohmigod', 'Fer sure', and 'That's sooo grody.' Valley-Speak even generated the number one song on the charts: 'Valley Girl,' by Frank Zappa.

More recently, there was a brief focus on Long-Island-Speak when all three networks did movies on the Amy Fisher case and, for better or worse, tried to capture that dialect. Lung Guylin girls, we were told, wore red 'nel' polish, went out on the water in 'sell' boats and road into the city on the 'rellroad.' On rare occasion, they would even read poach-tree, which is not an easy piece of Lung Guylindese to figure out, so I'll give you a hint. Poach-tree is verse that rhymes.

In my view, Rhode Islandese is at least as rich as any of those. What makes it fascinating is that such a distinct dialect has come out of such a small place. One might expect dialects to come out of regions - like the south, or the west coast - but out of a smudge on the fast lane to Cape Cod? For those of you with short memories, that's how the Wall Street Journal once described us. Anyway, maybe our smallness is why our accent has been overlooked by the world's language recorders. It's time that ends.

So here is kind of dictionary. As you'll see, it's not Webster's. The approach is simple enough. First, I state a word of Rhode Islandese, spelling it as best I know how. Then, in most cases, I follow it by a somewhat playful definition. And finally, to give it context, I follow each definition with an imaginary quote showing how the word might be used. Those quotes make up the majority of the dictionary, and include many other Rhode Islandisms that don't have their own definition, so you'll find new local phrases in nooks and crannies everywhere. To repeat, this isn't Webster's.

I did my best to make the quotes sound like they were coming from people who speak hardcore Rhode Islandese. Do most Rhode Islanders speak that way? No. Similarly, most southerners don't say, "If you don't arn my shirt so I can look speer while I change my tar, I'll yale." And most valley girls did not begin every sentence with, "Ohmidgod, that's sooo grody; I mean, like - gag me with a spoon fer sure." Perhaps the best comparison is that most Rhode Islanders don't look like the people Don Bousquet so evocatively draws in his cartoons - though frankly I've seen a few who do. But by going to a bit of an extreme, I think Don captures some local truths that allow all of us to laugh at ourselves. I tried to do the same thing in this dictionary - I went to a bit of an extreme. In essence, I asked myself: "If those people in Don Bousquet's cartoons could talk, how would they sound?" Basically: How would Vinnie and Chevul sound? Or rather, how DO they sound? I went on to craft quotes from that idea, staying as true as I could to real hardcore Rhode Islandese, rather than lapsing into out-and-out parody.

As I went along, I found myself doing something I hadn't set out to do: weaving a second book inside the dictionary. You might call it a tongue-in-cheek chronicle of Rhode Island culture. In each quote, I tried to touch on a piece of what life in this state is about. I suppose you could refer to a lot of those pieces as local stereotypes. But there's truth in those stereotypes. We really do scramble to buy bread before snowstorms. An inordinate amount of legislators really did go to LaSalle, Providence College and Suffolk Law School. We do love vanity plates, and maybe I stretched the corruption thing a bit, but one or two of our public officials - and credit union officials - have indeed distinguished themselves in those areas.

I'm afraid that along the way I made a fair amount of local lawyer jokes, since lawyers do figure prominently into our affairs and culture, perhaps more so than in other places. I want to say right here that I count lawyers among my best friends. I have a brother who is a lawyer. So I should make something clear about those jokes up front. I meant every one of them. I was pretty hard on Rhode Island politicians, as well. The truth is, local politicians aren't so bad. Most are truly committed to building up Rhode Island. I admire many of them for caring enough to get involved. We in journalism don't give local politicians nearly the credit they are due. And I meant every one of those jokes, as well.

As for the the made-up quotes I use to illustrate local word use, don't blame me for all of them. The truth is that I did not make up some of those that may sound most incredible. Take the word "Slanda," which of course is Rhode Island for slander. My quote for that one is as follows: "My opponent accuses me of being anti-Italian, but that's slanda. You want proof? I eat suppa rat Angelo's all the time. I love the gvayvy." Someone accused of being anti-Italian in Rhode Island really did say that - and said the last two sentences word for word. Actually, maybe it was the last three sentences. Someone in Rhode Island also said "God is a Democrat." That comes under the word, "Vih-tree."

This isn't the first time there's been an in depth attempt to capture Rhode Islandese on paper. Elaine Chaika, Professor of Linguistics at Providence College, has chronicled it in a number of papers, including an excellent effort sponsored both by the Providence Public Library and the National Endowment for the Humanities. Prof. Chaika calls our dialect "r-less." Or, as she herself wrote down, "ah-less." But she was quick to add we often do end up adding r's to places where they don't belong, like the noted 'soder' example. She goes on to say something I found out myself when I began trying to capture Rhode Islandese: it's not an easy task. Prof. Chaika's words: "The autha (her spelling) knows of no rules of simila complexity in any of the so-called 'r' pronouncing dialects of American English."

A confession: I couldn't figure out how to make sure that all the complex rules of Rhode Islandese applied to every word, phrase and sentence I used in this book, so let me offer an apology here and now to Prof. Chaika and other academic observers like her: this dictionary sure isn't perfect. I should offer the same apology to non-academics - which is to say everyone else who reads this - who may disagree with how I spelled words here and there. All I can say is I did my best. One alibi is that spoken dialects aren't easy to capture in written language. Well, maybe Mark Twain brought it off, but to parapharase Sen. Lloyd Bentsen, I'm no Mark Twain. I have another defense, too: there are sub-dialects within our dialect. In other words, people in Cranston speak slightly differently than people from Bristol, Narragansett, etc., etc. Or, to translate the word "etc." into Rhode Islandese: b'beep, b'bop, b'boop.

If Elaine Chaika wrote her treatise by rules, I'm afraid I wrote my own the same way I write columns: not from some well-thought out set of guidelines, but from the gut, or rather the ear in this case. Even so, it wasn't easy deciding how to spell many of the words. How, for example, do you spell the way Rhode Islanders say "here?" I tried "heeya," then "heea," and finally settled on "heah." That may not be perfect because some might read "heah" as stretching out that final "ah" sound the way farmers do in Maine. Most Rhode Islanders don't do it that way, except perhaps for the Swamp Yankees up in Glawsta and down South County way. We tend to say it fast, affecting the same sound as blurting the name "Mia" at lightning speed, not that I want to get into the Woody Allen mess heah.

Other pronunciations were even harder to spell - for example, the Rhode Island "ur" sound. As in perfect, nurse, work, hers and Journal. I played with it a bit and came down to two options: peuhfect or peahfect. Neither is perfect, but I went with "peuhfect." Or rather, "peuhfick." It seemed to follow in most cases: neuhse, heuhs, Jeuhnal. But I also found that with some words using this sound, like "early," the spelling didn't work at all. For me, seeing the word "euhly" on paper comes off as "yoo-lee." So I spelled it normally. Meanwhile, with a few "ur" sounding words, like homework, the "a" seemed to work better. This means I ended up with "homeweahk" on the one hand and "sheuhbeuht" on the other. Is that logical? Perhaps not, but again, I went by instinct and ear.

But even the "going by ear" technique didn't easily solve all problems. It's been observed, for example, that not only do we drop "r's" at the end of sentences, but often 't's" in the middle of them. It wasn't always simple to come up with a clear way to spell such pronunciations. Take the word "couldn't." How does a Rhode Islander say that? Kind of like "cou'int" but that only works if the apostrophe is read as a sharp break. Same with such words as "painting." I came up with "pai'ihn." That is not meant to be pronounced as payinn - it's more like pay-IHN, but again, with a kind of sharp break in the middle. The word "little?" That ended up as "lih'il." But my hope is that it won't be read as "lil." Try this for practice: "Mar'ihn is at a mee'ihn in the Nor'ihn Inn." As long as you break sharply at the apostrophes, it should work.

For a while, I did do my best to follow rules, but began to give up when I found that many are contradictory in Rhode Islandese. For example, in most cases, we tend to compress language, as in the noted case of "Have you eaten yet," which in our hands ends up being compressed into "Joozeet," or simply, "Jeet?" In Rhode Island, Italy becomes It-lee and Anthony becomes "Ant-knee." But in other cases, we stretch things out. "Sure" becomes "shoowa" and "door" becomes "do-wuh." By the same token, "store" becomes "sto-wuh." And arthritis it routinely stretched into "artheritis." Rules? What rules?

Even supposedly obvious pronunciations had some contradictions. One woman wrote me to say that Glocester is indeed pronounced as "Glawsta," but chiefly when used with "Fawsta," as in "No school Fawsta-Glawsta." In other contexts, she said, it would come off as "Glahsta." That was too much for me, so for consistency's sake, I've left it as "Glawsta" throughout.

Another tricky question was how to pronouce 'that?' Or hat, fat, sat, and bat. Some might have leaned toward 'theeat' and I did for a while - because in the lore of local language, we're suppose to add a few "e's" in front of every long "a" sound. As in the noted "Creeeeanston." So, in the early stages of this project, I did try "theeat." But it began to sound like a Brooklyn cab-driver - more like New Yorkese than Rhode Islandese - so I dropped it.

There's also a debate on when to add "r's" where they don't belong. As in "law" becoming "lawr." There are those who have very specific rules on that: you should only add the "r" when the next word begins with a vowel: "The lawr is a joke." But not when followed by a con-sonant: "The law must be obeyed." Again, I went by ear and ended leaving the r in all the time: "lawr."

There were other inconsistencies to explore: why does "North Kingstown" always come out as "North Kingston," but "Middletown" never comes out as "Middleton"? I did extensive re-search into this and have come up with the definitive answer. I have no idea.

At last, there was the great issue of how to spell "Rhode Island" itself in dialect. Many speak it in such a clipped way it compresses the whole first word down to almost nothing. So you could argue for a spelling that would look this way: ''R'Dyelin.'' But in the end, I went by ear and fell back on what has more or less become the accepted dialect spelling: ''Roe Dyelin.''

By the way, I'm not the only one who goes by ear in trying to capture our dialect. Most readers who wrote me composed their entire letters in Rhode Islandese - not just their suggestions - and each had their own various spellings. It was always a surprise to see who got caught up in the question of how we speak.

I got one letter from Susan Farmer, head of Channel 36. She signed it, ''Susan Fama.''

Jane Civins, administrative Associate of the Rhode Island Committee for the Humaninites wrote this: ''Mock! Ah aumos took a fit when I sawr yaw ahticle on RhoDislan Eze.''

Most correspondents addressed me as ''Mock.'' Some of the letters may have missed a sound or two but they were still classics renditions of local-speak.

''We yoosta live in Providence yiiz ago,'' wrote one reader. ''In the summuh, we yoosta go downrivvuh fuh kuppluh weeks in Rivviside aw K'nimikit.''

Another: ''So Mock, I jus had ta write this letta to letcha know I've been readin' watcha been wri'in.''

Yet another: ''Despite this beauteeful day, the fact remains that my cah has a dead battry and my typerider don't work. I recanized dis ammejutlee when I was leeavin' the house wit my wife to tork wit my brudder.''

A Rhode Island nurse name Allie Cullen sent me a humorous article she'd written for a professional journal chronicling some of the ways patients mangle the language in general - like the one who complained of a Sinai infection in the nose and face - but she also had plenty of Rhode Islandisms in there, including the way we refer to Tyelonol as ''Tie-noll.'' Or rather, ''the Tie-nolls.'' She went on to observe, much to my own benefit, how often we add a ''the'' in front of many things, particularly hospitals. It's not ''Kent Hospital.'' It's ''The Kent.'' Likewise, it's ''The Miriam,'' and even ''The Roe Dyelin.''

Another letter was signed, ''The Cawya Family,'' followed by the words, ''You figure the spelling.'' I'm guessing it's from the Coia family.

Every letter had suggestions of words, and I used scores to bolster my own list, though I did leave out a few so as not to hurt feelings. Like: ''New Yawt Times: Definition - Cheap imitation of the Providence Journal-Bulletin.'' I just couldn't do it to them down in Manhattan. Their egos are too fragile.

By the way, many letter writers ended up clipping out and sending me the same two ads to illustrate Rhode Islandese. One was for The Arcade and featured the slogan, "The Shopper Image." The letter writers all said they at first thought it was an ad for the high end catalogue, "The Sharper Image." Frankly, so did I. The point is that in Rhode Island, even the best slogans can end up only being confusing if they stumble over our dialect. The second example of this phenomenon - also sent in by many readers - is the well-known bumper sticker meant to be a play on words: "In RI, Drunk Drivers Get Court." Now - does that really mean "court?" Or does it mean "caught" - which is, after all, pronounced "court" in Rhode Island?

Incidentally, were this an academic text, I'd have to put an "*" at the end of that last paragraph and cite just which agencies put out those slogans. But it's not an academic text, so I won't, and besides, in Rhode Islandese, there's no such thing as an asterisk anyway. It's an astrick.

I'd like to make a last point on the text here. I can't overlook the truth that many of the phrases I use are national. Teenagers everywhere tend to say, "Sup," instead of "What's up?" And they also say "Wicked," though perhaps not quite the way our teenagers say it. Still, such phrases are so much a part of local speech patterns I ended up including them.

One problem for writers of long projects like this is knowing when to let go. I think I've got a reasonably good list of Rhode Island words here, but were I to think on it - or tap the thoughts of others - I could come up with a few new ones every day. So when does a Rhode Island dictionary writer stop? There came a point when I knew I had to.

A delivery man came to my home. For the previous three hours, I'd been working on this book in a home office. I had to write the man a check, and the total came to $47. I began to fill out the check. As I did, suddenly, I caught myself writing the words, "Fawty-seven." This really happened. Then something worse happened. I'm one of those people who keep lists of "things-to-do" on 3-by-5 cards. My problem is I have a habit of setting those cards aside and never looking at them again. So I left myself a big note on a yellow pad by the kitchen telephone to remind me. Only I found myself writing it down this way: "Check cods." Someone once said you know you've really learned a foreign language when you've begun to think in it. Similarly, you know you're really a Rhode Islander when you've begun to write in Rhode Islandese.

So I'll stop, and I think it's appropriate to end this where we began - on the quandary of why Rhode Islandese hasn't gotten the same attention as other national dialects - particularly southern dialect, which is currently in the White House? It even brings up a question: is America progressive enough, open-minded enough, tolerant enough, to vote a Rhode Island accent into the White House? Let's explore the possible result, on the steps of Congress, during the inauguration speech of the first potential Rhode Islander elected president:

"Mista chief justice, forma prezdints, assawted sentas, mayas and my fella Americans. Howai-iya? I stand heah as a humble cih'azin who springs not from wealth, but a mih'il class family from Harxie Faw Cawniz. My election is not one cannadit's vih-tree, but ratha mocks the mavitch of a new co-lition, a new pottnaship between ah potties. The dilemmers we face ah lodge ones and the anssis will be hod to find. We cannot be global pleecemin, but ah food kuhbbids must be open to the paw. So let us be caffle in this un-seuhtin weuhld, but let us embvace the few-tcha with spivvit and feuhva. Afta all, t'mahrra is oz. This time in histree is the American owwa. Let us not be prizznizz of ah fate. Let us be seeve-ee-us about ah weahk but have a sense of yuma about ahselves. Two-bee onnis witcha, this is summa in Americker, so let us go fawth with ennigee, as leadiz in a time of followiz. I thank you and ask f'yaw prazz."

On second thought, I'm not shoo-wa America's ready for us after all.

A WORD ABOUT THE ANECDOTES PLACED THROUGHOUT THE DICTIONARY

I quickly found a problem trying to capture the range of Rhode Islandese through a traditional dictionary format alone: part of appreciating our accent comes from reading true stories about how it's been used - and misused. So I came upon the idea of writing short anecdotes to illustrate that. I had a rich selection to choose from: many readers sent in tales of their encounters with the accent. And in conversation - personal and business- I've come across many other such tales. So I wrote them up, and put them in this book. The names I included are real.

I also came upon a writing device to help emphasize just how different our accent is - the device of made-up conversations between a Rhode Islander and a Non-Rhode Islander. I crafted a number of such made-up conversations and put those in here, too.

One of the most amusing - and telling - anecdotes I came across about our accent was sent to me by Irene Townley Day, wife of the noted Rhode Island cartoonist Chon Day. She wrote to tell me of visiting her husband's family in New Jersey. They were so fascinated by how she as a native Rhode Islander spoke that they actually asked her to repeat four particular phrases so they could hear again and again the idiosyncrasies of our speech. The phrases: 1. Park your car. 2. A purple bird sat on a curbstone. 3. New Jersey. And, 4. Over there.

I'll let you come up with the Rhode Island pronunciations. Meanwhile, let that be the first anecdote about Rhode Islandese, and the start of this chronicle of how we speak.

A

ACK'CHILI: A word emphasizing the truth. ''Ack'chili, most Roe Dylandas bleeve you're spoze-ta speed up on yelliz. And pass on the right.''

ADDA BURRA: Massachusetts city just nawta P'tucket. ''I had a choice of relocay'in in eitha my pottnaship's Wes'tuhly branch aw the Adda Burra branch. Bleeve me, Adda Burra would be much eazia. Wes'tuhly's 20 miles feuhtha from Prahvdince and uses maw gazoleen. But at least it's not ova the state line. I cou'int handle leavin' Roe Dyelin evvyday. So I took Wes'tuhly.''

AH FATHA: Stot of Lawd's Pre'a. ''I stopped bein' religious when I left the state, but now that I'm back, I've begun to say an 'Ah Fatha' tree, faw, figh times a day. Awliss at the same times. Right befaw I begin drivin' on Roe Dyelin roads.''

AH: Letta found between 'Q' and 'S' in alphabet. This proved unacceptable to mayoral candidate Ralph Russo of Johnston who feahed a last name beginning wit 'ah' would push him too fah down the alphabetical ballot. So he legally added an 'A.' He's still in orfuss. ''My sista-'n-lawr down at the cawthouse tole me Ahleen was in yesstay changin' heuh name to aViolet. Guess she's runnin'.''

AH: Our. Not to be confused with the letta 'ah.' ''Ah state is the only one that begins wit ah.''

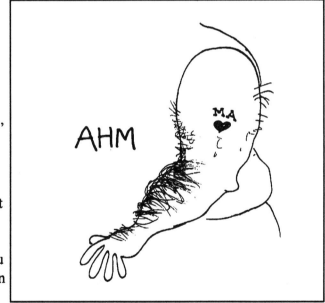

AHM: Body part leading to the fingas. ''You crazy? You bruised y'ahm and y'not puh'in in f'comp? My Uncle Ahtha's been collectin' six months faw a bruised ahm. Not to mention my brothin-lawr B'nahd who twisted 'iz shoulda when Prezdint Fawd was in orfuss. He's been collectin' evva since. If you wanna talk to him about it, he's weahking out at the gym today.''

AHRINGE: Color of uppa Bay. ''I like t'wash down my Jonnycakes wit ahringe juice. Except when I have cawfee milk. Though sometimes I just head to the Creamree and wash down breh'fiss wit an Orful-Orful. A lodge a'cawse.''

AIGS: Eggs. ''The main reason I luv Roe Dyelin is you can bveake the aigs in half at the staw and buy only six. Or even faw. Try that in any otha state. I luv the bay, too, and the beaches, but it's mostly what they letcha do wit the aigs.''

AIHS: What Bellevue Avenue residents are felt to be putting on. ''I don't know about Chevul these days; she's been puh'ihn on aihs evva since that N-G boyfriend of heuhs Vinnie got that Lumina Z34. Evvy time you talk to heuh, it's 'dual twin cam V6' this, and '210 hawses unda th'hood' that, and I can't take it anymaw.''

AIRS: Made routinely by P'tucket Red Sox infeel. ''A'cawse we make ah sheah a' airs. Why-ja think weah down heah instedda Fenway? The Pawdogs?''

AMBLINZ: A vehicle known to be chased on occasion by seuhtin Roe Dyelin loyiz. ''Right afta the EMT's put me in the amblinz, they said they needed the name of my docta. I said, 'F'get my docta. Call my loya. And tell him right off it's a dream case: low-a back, and soft tissue.' ''

Soon after Phyllis Boucher moved to Rhode Island 30 years ago, a neighbor mentioned that her husband had been in the 'Aihcaw.''

Phyllis processed that for a few minutes, then thought she understood. The neighbor had meant "Echo." Back then, it struck Phyllis that something called the "Echo" was probably a publication - a service publication.

She began asking about what the husband's role had been on the publication.

Now it was the neighbor's turn to be confused. But she figured it out soon and set Phyllis straight.

"No, no," the neighbor corrected. "Air Corps."

AMEEJITLEE: Pronto. ''Lissen to me, young lady. I'm y'motha, and just because I'm an indulgent, Yuppie, Easside, baby boom pearint doesn't mean I don't know how to drawr lines wit my own faw-yeea-old dawda. I want you upsteahs ameejitlee, and I'm not gonna take no faw an ansa. This is y'last chance. I'm going t'count to 1,500...''

ANKA: Symbol on state seal. Also, Doug White. ''My lih'il Teddy's awready readin' the Stah and Nashnil Enkwiya rat the supamocket - speshlee the murda and Bigfoot stahries. I just know he's gonna anka the 6 and 11 on channel 12 when he groze up.''

ANSISS: Answers. "You wou'int bleeve the ansiss they gave me evvy time I went into a restrint in Illinoise and asked faw a grinda and cab'nit: 'Sahree ma'am. You want the hodweah staw 'round the cawna.'"

ANT-KNEE: First name of former State Treszhuh. "How come I cou'int find Ant-Knee's name on the ballot this time? I thought he was Treszhah faw life."

ANTALUZ: Pot of male deea. "Neks week is huh'in season. Waddayasay we hit Prudence wit ah boze-n-arriz and bring home some trophy bucks wit antaluz? Though if we miss, I have a waita friend at Bugaboo Creek who knows how to awda some through a catalog - awready mounted. Annee promises he won't tell anyone so we can claim we bagged 'em ahselves. Though it could be a problem if they stot talking up theah on the trophy wall while companeeze ova."

ANKA

ASHFAWT: Used by state DOT workers' to pave friends' driveways year round, as well as all state roads the month before elections. "Jimmy Hoffer? Definitely not alive, that's f'shoowa. My guess is he's somewheah deep in the ashfawt. Though not in any Roe Dyelin Route 95 overpasses, because he'd have fallen outta the cracks by now."

AVVAGOODWON: Adios. "Niceseenya. Gotta run. I'm goin up th'house. Waddaya mean y'don't unnastand? 'I'm goin up th'house' is Roe Dyelin faw 'I'm goin home.' Avvagoodwon."

Mary Jemail is now living in New York city, but still considers herself a displaced Newporter; that's where her family is from. Her mother used to get her hair done by a local stylist who one day announced he was moving from Newport. She asked where, but didn't understand his answer. His Rhode Island accent was so heavy it was even hard for a fellow Rhode Islander like her to grasp.

So she asked him to repeat it. "Oddick," he said. She asked if that was in Rhode Island. Of course, he said, and then repeated it once more: "Oddick." At last, she asked him to write it down. He did.

Of course. Over the bridges. Up 95. In West Warwick.

Arctic.

The Rhode Island Dictionary

AW-WUTT?: Or what? Used at end of a sentence. "Weah spose-lee friends since we w'kids, then I found out he put my name down faw a loan I nevva took out at 'iz creh-it union and grabbed the money faw 'imself. When I confronted him, he tells me to calm down and have a muffin. The next week, he disapeeiz. Is he a bum aw-wutt?"

AWDA: What you do after the waitress comes to your table. "I'd like to awda a chowda, lodge grinda, french fries wit vinega and a vaniller cab'nit pleece. I'd also like six clamcakes and a plate a' stuffies. And a big awda of zepolle. Now - waddaya got faw entrees?"

AWLISS: Always. "I awliss put out my lawn deea, blue reflective lawn globe and ceramic bend-ova goddna rat the feuhst sign of Spring. Doesn't evvyone in Roe Dyelin? Oh, did I mention my wood goose onna stick wit wings that spin in the breeze?"

AYYY: Nice to see you. Stot of 45 peuhcent of all sentences spoken by Roe Dyelin teenagers. "Ayyy, Vinnie. Yo. Long time. Waddaya say we check out the hot bod contest at Shootiz this Saddy?"

The Rhode Island Dictionary

B

B'BEE, B'BAH, B'BOO: Etc. "If we hit the Creamree feust and Ben 'n Jevvee's seh'ind, we'll have ah pick of evvy flayva evva made: strawbree, rasbree, moaker, sheuhbeuht, peppamint, pistarchio, cawfee, ahmind, mobble brownie, ahreo, bannaner, peana' butta, moshmellow, Cherry Gahcia, wartamelon, sossprilla, chawclit, vaniller, fudgicles, b'bee, b'bah, b'boo."

B'ZAH: Bizarre. "My friends from outtastate keep tellin' me it's a b'zah way to make a living, but I just tole them, 'Geddout.' I mean, what's so b'zah? Evvyone I know in Roe Dyelin wants to be a Keno writa."

BA'DAY'DAH: Dan Quayle had trouble spelling this word. "Extra butta and sowwa cream f'my baked ba'day'dah, pleece, but make it a Diet Coke; I'm watchin' my weight."

BA-BING, BA-BING: Pronto. "Y'want me to recommend a good resstrint neah the mall? A minute by cah? So you can go right back to shoppin'? I see - you want to go 'Ba-bing, ba-bing' - right? Try Casser Lupiter."

BA BA

BABA: Cuts haia. "Don't evva call me a baba again. I'm a bawd-ceahtified cosmetologist, witta licensed sub-speshatee in ova-moussed big haia. Last yeea, at the Roe Dyelin haia-stylist's convention, I got the golden Cockatiel awahd. By the way, I put the Cockatiel trophy at my cuttin' station, and now evvy geuhl who comes in says, 'That's the cut I want.' "

BAH'UL: The glass container that milk, juice and beeya comes in. "C'nighve a bah'ul uh 'Gansett. Huh? They don't make it anymaw? No problem, how 'bout a Budweisa? Y'otta that? A Milla then? No? Okay, a Caw's Lite? Outta that, too? I'll juss go with wine, then. How 'bout a nice bah'ul a shadnay.''

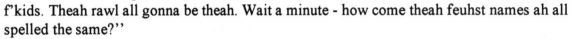

BAHNEE: Barney. "I've got a 2, 4, and 6-yeea-old. The only time I get outta the house is to go to my weekly suppawt group f'pearints who have to lissen to Bahnee-the-Dinasaw on TV two owwas a day.''

BAH'UL

BAHNEE: Bonnie. "Gonna be a soopa potty. It's bein' thrown by Ole Stone Bank. Bahnee Frank is the speaka, Bahnee Raitt the singa, Bahnee Rubble the entataina f'kids. Theah rawl all gonna be theah. Wait a minute - how come theah feuhst names ah all spelled the same?''

BAT'REECE: Source of powwa for the Enna-jiza bunny. "My radio's outta bat'reece, and my motha won't give me anymaw 'cause she says we might need them faw a heuh'cane. How'm I gonna lissen to P-R-O wit Chevul during lunch in the cafterier?''

BATTROOM: What Roe Dyelin females visit in packs at restrinz. "Dju bleeve the lines outside the ladies battroom at Trinty? Not to mention at the Prahvdince P'fawming Ott Senta. I havvent seen the seh'in act theah in 10 yizz.''

BEH'UH: Better. "I've stopped callin' radio tawk shows evvy day, have begun to drive a half owwa to restrinz at night, havvent touched cawfee milk in a month and have quit plane Keno evvy time I go to the cawna stowuh. Sheesh. I'd beh'uh sign up faw some Roe Dyelin refresha cawses - I'm obviously losing touch wit my local heah-tij.''

BIW CLIH'IN: Fawty-seh'in Prezdint. "It's weeihd havin' a commanda-in-chief wit such a funny axxent, innit?''

BIWFO: Wallet. "My grandfatha's been goin' nuts evva since he lost 'iz biwfo. He had figh-hunnit dollis innit, but that's not the problem. The problem is 'iz seenya citizen's RIPTA cod. He loves savin' that 50 cents a ride.''

BLAH - KYELIN

BLAH-KYELIN: Accessible by ferry. ''Ak-chili, Blah-keylin's a lot like Roe Dyelin; it's small, insula, and evvyone does deals wit people they know.''

BLENDA: Common appliance, often found neah the dishwasha, toasta, Mixmasta, knife shoppana, 'letrick can opena, Amaner rayda range, food steama, juice extracta, Kweezanot, and pahster mayka. ''I bought my wife Brender a Blenda and she's goin' nuts making the offical Roe Dyelin shake. Cawfee cab'nits.''

BLINDA: Used around hawses' eyes by the Prahvdince mounted pleece. ''My hawse Caspa heah was 'speshlee trained t'chase any cah that slides a stop sign. Thank goodness he's got extra-lodge blindas on aw we'd be chasin' evree cah in Roe Dyelin.''

BLINKA: What Rhode Island motorists nevva use. ''The sales guy said standit items include cruise control, eea, powwa windows, tape deck and cellula phone, but Roe Dyelin's the one state wheah blinkas ah optional.''

BLOW: Opposite of 'above.' ''Guy on Prime Time Live said the ethical standits in Roe Dyelin ah blow average, but my cousin the state senta - who got me my job as head of Public Weahks - says Prime Time's fulla'it.''

BOAT: Both. ''Chevul and I ah goin to Awlando, Flahrida togetha this winna. We've weahked hod building weahka's comp cases and we boat deseuhve a nice warta-skiin' hollday.''

Rler: "So you're new in town."

Non-Rler: "Just arrived."

Rler: "You'll haffta come with me to a bake this weekend; sample some cakes."

Non-Rler: "You mean like a local Betty Crocker bake-off?"

Rler: "Beh'ee Crocka? Well, a bake anyway. At the shaw. Have some cakes."

Non-Rler: "This is some form of bakeoff - right?"

Rler: "I spose. But with seaweed and rocks."

Non-Rler: "That's how you cook cakes around here?"

Rler: "It's the only way."

Non-Rler: "You don't just do it in the stove with a pan?"

Rler: "Gedaddaheah. Weah talkin diggin' an eight-inch pit and linin' it with rocks, puh'ihn wood inside and beuhnin' it f'tree owwas, then rakin' that out so you can fill it with seaweed. Afta that's when y'begin bakin'. When it's steamin' real good, you covva it all with canvass."

Non-Rler: "Chocolate cakes on seaweed and rocks?"

Rler: "Who said anything about chawklit cakes?"

Non-Rler: "I thought you said I should sample some local cakes."

Rler: "Clamcakes. At a clambake."

Non-Rler: "Oh. What are clamcakes?"

Rler: "I'm afraid you have a lot to leuhn about Roe Dyelin."

The Rhode Island Dictionary

BOLLYBAW: A net spawt. Like bad-mih'in, but with maw playiz and a bigga baw. ''We do it evvy Sundy - go to Guardid Pock, play bollybaw and eat macroni and meatbaws. Doesn't evvy Roe Dyelin famlee?''

BRARERS: Plural of brassiere. ''Dju bleeve the brarers Madonna waw on heuh last toowa? Heuh paw motha. I'll tell ya this: that's one young lady who dih'int lissen to the sistas.''

BREH'FISS: What you eat afta y'mornin showwa. ''I awliss stot my day witta fruit bowl of bannaners, guavers and papayers ova carttidge cheese. That kinda breh'fiss is impawtant to me as a Roe Dyelinda. It gives me a chance to pronounce the letta ''ah'' faw a change.''

BROONS: Local hockey team. ''People say theah's nuh'ihn mayja league in Roe Dyelin, but that's not true. Theah's a lot heah. The Broons faw example. Theah's uppa bay pollution. And the Rocky Point Shaw Dinna Hall. That's tree mayja league things right theah. And I haven't even begun to talk about ah landfills.''

Rler: "I think I'm gonna bveak up with Motty. He's not very polite anymaw. I don't like his b'hayve'ya at all."

Non-Rler: "What's that word?"

Rler: "B'hayve'ya. You know. The way he ax."

Non-Rler: "Ax?"

Rler: "His manniz."

Non-Rler: "What are manniz?"

Rler: "He's got bad manniz. He ax like a while baw."

Non-Rler: "What's a 'while baw'?"

Rler: "Like a pig.'

Non-Rler: "Oh - a wild boar."

Rler: "That's what I said. A while baw. I won't stand f'that kinda b'hayve'ya."

Non-Rler: "What's b'hayve'ya again?"

BUBBLA: Sole source of drinkable water in P'tucket...except for those brave enough to drink from forcetts. ''She asked me wheah the fountain was. 'In the pock in Kennedy Plaza,' I said. She said, 'No, the fountain.' I said, 'I juss tole ya; in the pock.' She said, 'No, a fountain like whatcha drink outta.' I said, 'You mean the bubbla?' She said, 'What's a bubbla?' Obviously an outtastayta.''

BUH'IN: What political candidates stot handin' out 23 months befaw th'election. ''If I were you I'd keep that buh'in. And 'iz bumpa sticka, too. They'll be collectiz items soon as he gets indicted.''

BUH-IN

VOTE VINCENT A MANCINI

BULLAVOD: Prime address on Easside. No need to use full name; it's simply, 'The Bullavod.' ''Weah trine to get a system set up wit the city rekwiya'in anyone who lives west of Hope Street to show passes befaw theah allowed to cross east of it. And also to ban all but rezdints and guests from The Bullavod itself. I mean, if weah gonna keep up Easside proppity values, we've simply got to insulate, insulate, insulate.''

BUTTA: Higher in klestrole than mahjrin. ''If y'put anymaw butta on those dough-boys, y'gonna need an angioplasty befaw dezeuht. And if y'keep eatin' 'em evvyday, you'll look like a human veuhsion of a Don Bousquet cahtoon.''

Duane Firth moved to Rhode Island with his family in 1967. At one point, he decided he needed to go out and buy some building materials for various jobs. He happened to mention it in passing to several people, and all told him the same thing: He should check out "Bruce DeLumba."

Duane presumed Bruce was a handyman who could help him with the work. He was impressed that so many people immediately thought of the same guy for such jobs.

It was only later that he realized they were directing him to a retail outlet called Brewster Lumber.

Martha Crossley is a transplanted Rhode Islander from New Jersey. Tongue-in-cheek, she points out that as New Jerseyans, she and her husband were already comfortable with such Rhode Island concepts as organized crime, kickbacks and landfill woes. But certain quirks were new to her. Like local language.

For example, she promptly noticed that few things here were simply "good" - they were "wicked good." Or rather, "wickit good.' Soon, Martha and her husband found themselves using the phrase themselves. Dinner, they told each other, was wickit good, and so was the movie. It was a wickit good game, and on some days, the weather was truly wickit, wickit good.

She took a marketing position at Hasbro, and early on, asked some associates if there was a water fountain on site. She was told that Hasbro didn't splurge on such unnecessary items. Puzzled, she went on to explain that she was thirsty and wondered where she could get a drink of water. At that, she was directed to something called a "bubbla." She wasn't quite sure what that was, but followed the directions and lo and behold, came upon a water fountain.

At least a half dozen Rhode Islanders who ended up being transplants sent in tales of an opposite kind of 'bubbla' story, which is to say they themselves knew what it meant but no one else did.

Jim, a Rhode Islander by birth, was working in California when he asked his new colleagues if there was a bubbla nearby. They all looked at him as if he'd come from Mars until one simply said, "We don't have anything like that." Jim went back to work, soon did find a bubbler, and pointed it out to his colleagues. "We call that a water fountain," one said.

Jim said he would remember that. "A warta fountain," he repeated. They looked at him funny again, but let it go.

Cashier in California grocery: "I'm sorry sir, you'll have to get the rest of the package. You can't buy one stick of butter."

Rler: "Geddout."

Non-Rler: "There's no need to threaten me, sir."

Rler: "Everyone bize-a stick atta time in Roe Dyelin."

Non-Rler: "I'm sorry sir. We have different rules here. You'll have to get the rest of the package."

Rler: "Can I goat the butta aisle wittout losin' my place?"

Non-Rler: "Goat?"

Rler: "Goat th'aisle."

Non-Rler: "What do you mean, 'goat' sir."

Non-Rler: "Goat the butt'aisle."

Rler: "Buttile? Sir?"

Rler: "I won't then."

Non-Rler: "Sir, you have to go back to the butter section."

Rler: "I juss hax you that."

Non-Rler: "Hax?"

Rler: "Uh-huh. A seh'ihn ago."

Non-Rler: "Whatever, sir. And while you're back there, you'll have to get the other half of these eggs. You're not allowed to break an egg carton in two."

Rler: "Geddout."

Non-Rler: "If you threaten me again sir, I'll be forced to call security."

Rler: "I always break the cottin in two back home."

Non-Rler: "That's fine, sir, but we're not talking about cottin. We're talking about eggs. You can't break an egg carton in half."

Rler: "But I only need a few aigs."

Non-Rler: "I repeat, sir - you can't break an egg carton in half."

Rler: "Y'shoo-wa?

Non-Rler: "Pardon sir?"   (Continued)

The Rhode Island Dictionary

Rler: "Y'shoo-wa?"

Non-Rler: "I don't understand sir, but you'll have to get the rest of the butter box and the egg carton."

Rler: "Geddout."

Non-Rler: "I warned you sir."

Rler: "Okay. I'll goat the butta and aig eavias right now."

Non-Rler: "Ee-vee-uz, sir?"

Rler: "Eavias. You know, sections. Aisles. You want me to get the resta the butta and the cottin? Consida it done."

Non-Rler: "Not the cottin, sir. The eggs."

Rler: "Right. But I'll say one thing about Calaphonia. It's one b'zah state."

C

CAB'NIT: Popular at the Creamree. "No wonda Biw Clih'in's overweight. Paypa says he 'az cab'nit sessions twice a day."

CAFFLE: What P'tucket May-a Brian Sarault wasn't while pocketing kickbacks. "Gotta be caffle who you take bribes from in this state. It's an awful comment on values out theah. Y'just nevva know who's wea'ing a why-a."

CAH: Lodge, four-wheeled device for displaying vantee plates. Also, what locals nevva drive more than figh miles to restrinz in. "I got this gift seuhtifikit to the Red Roosta, but jeesh, that's all the way down Nawt Kingston way. And I live in Prahvdince. No chance. A' cawse, if we could find a cheap motel neah-bye so we wou'int half to drive theah and back the same night, I'd consida it."

CAH

CAMBLEEVE: The inability to accept a truth or event. "I cambleeve it. I pocked my new cah right between two spaces at Ann in Opes and I still got my daw scratched. Next time I take up tree spaces."

CANDITZY: Candidacy. "A'cawse I'm suppaw'ihn 'iz canditzy. His policies ah right, it's time faw a change, he's got vision, and most impaw'int, he promised a job to my brothin-lawr."

CARL ITCH: Institute of hiya education. "Weah so proud of Mahgrit faw geh'in into the carl itch of heuh choice, but it's breakin ah hots that she'll be leavin' Prahvdince. We hope she'll visit once aw twice a yeea. She's goin' all the way to Rahja Williams in Bristol."

CAWDA: Hallway. "He was the most earnest kid in high school. They even made him a hall monitta. All mawning long, he'd sit theah and say the same thing: 'You wanna go down the cawda, you'll need a haw pass.' Haw pass, haw pass, haw pass. Most earnest kid I evva met. I should've known Jack Reed would grow up to be the most earnest congressman in D.C.''

CAWFEE: Official state flavoring. ''Feuhst I tole 'em, 'Let's stop in this sto-wuh - evvything's on special.' He says, 'What's that mean?' I say, 'On special, on special - evvything's on special.' He still doesn't get it. Fine-lee I say, 'On sale.' That he undastands. Then I say, 'Let's go to caw-fee.' He says, 'What's that?' I say, 'To caw-fee, to cawfee, - let's go to cawfee.' He still doesn't get it. Fine-lee, I say, 'Let's take a break.' That he undastands.' We get to the cawfee shop, and I say, 'I think I'll just have a cawffee milk. You?' He says - 'No, I take mine black.' I don't think he's from around heah.''

CAWNA STO-WUH: Also know as 'Milk Sto-wuh,' ''A new outfit from New Yawk put a cawna sto-wuh in ah naybahood, but it went unda in six munts. The problem was theah milk section. It had one shelf f'whole, one f'skim and one f'chawclit, but they nevva figya'd out that around heah, you need a whole 'nutha shelf f'cawfee milk.''

CHAHZ-TIN: Pot of Sow County. ''I don't keah what the pleece say about evacu-ay'ihn befaw the heuhcane. This is my beachfront carttidge. My grandfatha built it. The shaw is my home. If the ocean d'sides to come into it, I'm gonna be heah to shovel it right back out. Real Roe Dyelindas don't evacuate.''

Jeanette Nessett moved to Rhode Island from Connecticut ten years ago. She was trained as a dietician, but couldn't find work in her field right away, so she did some waitressing while job-hunting.

She was still new in the state at this point and hadn't picked up much local dialect. So she was puzzled one day when a customer asked if they had cabinets in the restaurant. Wanting to be polite, Jeanette tried to answer as best she could.

"Well sure," she said. "I mean in the kitchen we store things in cabinets. Why do you ask?"

The customer starting laughing. "You're not from Rhode Island," he said, "are you?"

She said she wasn't. Patiently, he offered up what turned out to be her first of many lessons in Rhode Islandese.

CAWNA STAW

CHEUHCH: A word usually prefaced by 'The' in Roe Dyelin. "Me? Same routine as all Roe Dyelindas. Cheuhch Sundy mawn-ins', bowlin' at Cvann-stin Bowl Sundy aftanoons."

CHEVUL: Female name. "Me 'n Chevul were plann'n to spend the day at Midlin Mall, but heuh big haia went limp, so we had t'go home early.

CHIGONNA: What are you going to? "'Chiggona do this Saddy? How about we put on ah shoppist neckchains and check the babes at Skahbruh? I mean - babes do like neckchains on men, right?"

CHEVUL

CHINER: Located south of Mongolier. "My husband's a vettrin. He fought in the Chiner-Beuhmer-Indier theata deuring Weahld Waw II. Because of that, I think he pvounced maw 'ah's' during his faw yizz in the seuviss than in the fawty-figh yizz since."

CHODGE: Purpose of plastic. "Does the Rej-stree let you pay faw van'tee plates witta chodge cod? Maw impawtent, if I close a private deal faw a two-digit Roe Dyelin plate, will the bank give me a mawckgidge to pay faw it?"

CHOWDA: Neks to coffee milk and lemonade slush, Roe Dyelin's third most popula liquid food group. "My grandfatha Elma still makes the best chowda in the state. Evree August, he goes downcella and steuhs up 20 gallons: clams, clam juice, uny-

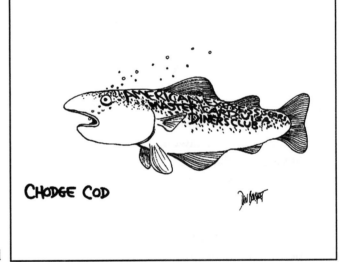

CHODGE COD

inz, ba'day'diz, and salt pawk. He gets the whole famlee to spend the week befaw diggin' ko-hogs at the shaw, then we shuck'em and he goes to it. It's a secret resspee, but if you don't tell anyone, he also puts in black peppa, white peppa and cayenne peppa. Then he puts in posslee stems and cream & butta. Some people like t'maytiz, but not Gramper Elma. And he doesn't use any food processa eitha; he chops evvything wit the same hatchet he uses to kill chickens. He's nevva written the resspee down, but alwiss tells us: 'If you don't rememba anything else, rememba the salt pawk.' And he's got no problem if y'want t'add y'own gollick powda and wissta sauce. Oh, and by the way: gramper has no time f'people who make it the red, New Yawk way and call it chowda. Blasphemy, he says. In his book, red chowda isn't chowda. It's warta.''

CLEANSAS: Where Rhode Island women have hair-mousse stains drycleaned off blouse shouldiz. ''She asked what she could do about heuh dirty cloze, and I said, 'Cleansas.' She said, 'No, it's my cloze I wanna clean, not the kitchen sink.' I said, 'Cleansas.' She said, 'Y'not lissn'n, I don't want Ajax, I want a laundr'mat.' I said, 'Right. The cleansas.' It still dih'int rej-ster. New Yawkas. Don't they know anything?''

CLUBBIN: A hip Roe Dyelanda's phrase for making the rounds of local nightlife. ''Ayyy - Frankie. Like I know Shootiz is cool, and Sh'Booms too, and if yaw' an Easside Yuppie, the Hot Club is hip, but I heah theah geh'ihn' some vossity babes at D'meeary-ot Oh-tel these days. Like, mayja-league hot mamas. Waddaya say we check out the action t'mahrra night while weah clubbin'? Betta yet, les hit it New Yeea's eve when the ealines put up theah stews f'the night. It'll be shoo'in fish in a barrel. But do me a fayva; don't f'get yaw ID cod.''

COBBARAYTA: Located near the spock plugs. ''He said to me, 'Y'otta luck m'am; y'cobbarayta's shot and it'll take a week to get a new one.' I doan know, Bobbra, if I half t'go that long wittout my van'tee plates, I won't know who I am anymaw.''

COBBLA: Known as shoe repairman in otha states. ''He's my favrit cobbla - has a bubbla so you can drink warta while he fixes y'loafas. I had an outtastate friend viz-ztin and tole heuh weah stoppin at the cobbla's. She looks at me funny and says, 'Grow up. Gepetto was just a cahtoon char-acta.''

COLE DOWT: Description of outdoor temperature. ''Doesn't matta t'me how cole dowt it is; it can be ten blow and I'm still goin' to weahk. On th'otha hand, even if it's fawty-figh degrees, if I see one flaykiv snow, I'm leavin' the orfuss, headin' to the supamocket and stockin' up on bread and milk along wit th'rest a'th'state.

COMB: Popular way to awda ice cream at the Creamree. ''Two ice cream combs pleece, tree scoops on d'boata'em. And don't f'get the jimmies.''

COMPUTA: Accawdin to the state masterplan, they'll replace abacuses at the Mota Vee'kil Rej-stree by the late 90's. ''I juss gotta great computa from Leachmeah. Packid Bell 170 meggerbyte hod drive witta 14 inch monitta and built-in softwheah, includin' weuhd processsa and organiza. I love to show it off. Huh? How do I teuhn it on? This I don't know.''

COPPIT: Floor covering. ''If y'thinkin of openin' a coppit sto-wuh, do it in Johnston. I heah they have more shag p'squeah inch than any town this side a' Jeuhsey. But f'get the Easside. Those Yankees eat, breathe and sleep wood flaws. Besides, the richa they ah, the less they redeckrate.''

COPPITBAGGA: Anyone running for local orfuss who grew up anywheah but the Roe Dyelin town theah running in. ''Imagine that coppitbagga comin' into Newpawt and runnin' f'city council. He's an off-islanda f'goodness sakes. From nowheah close to heah. Grew up in Jamestown.''

Rler at an out-of-state restaurant: "A cabinet please."

Non-RI Waiter: "This isn't a furniture shop sir."

Rler: "A grinda, then."

Non-Rler: "Sir, I'm busy. This isn't a hardware store."

Rler: "A cawfee please."

Non-Rler: "Do you mean a cup of coffee?"

Rler: "Right, a cawfee."

Non-Rler: "I trust you mean a cup of coffee. I've never had anyone simply order 'a coffee.' "

Rler: "Right - a cuppa cawfee. Akchili, make that an ice cawfee."

Non-Rler: "This is December, sir. You want an iced coffee?"

Rler: "Sounds good to me. An ice cawfee."

Non-Rler: "Fine. I presume by 'ice coffee' you really mean 'iced coffee."

Rler: "I'd also like two gaggiz."

Non-Rler: "Pardon?"

Rler: "You know - gaggiz. Bellybustas."

Non-Rler: "I still don't follow you sir."

Rler: "Two weeniz."

Non-Rler: "Weeniz?"

Rler: "And it'd be great if you carry New Yawk systems."

Non-Rler: "This isn't a computer store, sir."

Rler: "Just give me a dynamite then, okay?"

Non-Rler: "We certainly don't carry dynamite."

(Continued)

The Rhode Island Dictionary

Rler: "Do you carry bah'day'diz?"

Non-Rler: "Not that I know of. Never heard of them."

Rler: "Every restrint does. French fried bah'day'diz pleece. And a bah'ul of vinega."

Non-Rler: "Vinegar? So you want a salad sir?"

Rler: "No salad."

Non-Rler: "Fine."

Rler: "But a bah'ul of vinega."

Non-Rler: "For what if not a salad, if I may ask?"

Rler: "Fries."

Non-Rler: "You want vinegar on French fries?"

Rler: "Only way to eat 'em."

Non-Rler: "I've had a long day sir."

Rler: "Fine, I'll make it easy on you. Just whip me up a tawpeeda sangwidge."

Non-Rler: "We don't carry those either sir, whatever they are."

Rler: "Okay, okay. Just bring me a cawfee milk and we'll call it a day."

Non-Rler: "One coffee with milk then?"

Rler: "No, a cawfee milk."

Non-Rler: "Right. A coffee with milk. Do you take sugar in that?"

Rler: "Les stot ova."

COVVUPT: What Prime Time Live made us famous for. ''It's bad enough they pay us state legislatas only $5 a day. Weuhss still, they make us take 'How-to-not-be-covvupt' classes explaining things like what a conflict-a-intrist is, as if I don't awready no. It's so demeaning. And how am I spoze-ta even make the classes when the mawning ones meet while I'm weahking as an auto deala and the aftanoon ones meet while I'm chairing my senate committee on setting new standits f'selling cahs? It's unfaia.''

CREANSTIN: Also pronounced Creanstin . Epicenter of Roe Dyelin dialect. ''Just got back from a month travlin' th'whole country. Calaphonia, Delaweea, Flahrider, Atlanter, Kanzis, Nawt Dakoter, Ahrigan - even Alasker. And I'll say one thing: am I glad to be back home in Cvann-stin around people who don't talk funny.''

CUM'BUH'LIN: P'tucket's Barrington. ''We were thinkin' of movin' from the Eas-side ovva to Cum'buh'lin, but that would make Chollie's commute 15 minutes - tree times longa than it is now. He said he cou'int handle all that time on the road, so weah stane put.''

Norman Tilles, now a Providence insurance executive, moved to Rhode Island in 1946 to take a job as assistant buyer with the Outlet Department store. Early on, he was rearranging a table-display of fabrics. He decided to move some bolts of rayon off the table and put on bolts of a different fabric instead. So he asked an assistant - a born Rhode Islander - if he'd go in the storage area and bring out some cartons so Norman could remove the rayon bolts.

"Cahttins?" said the assistant.

Tilles nodded. Yes, he wanted cartons.

A few minutes later, the assistant came out with several bolts of cotton fabric.

Rler: "You have any coals I can bahro? I'm takin' the family to Gaurdid Pock faw a picnic and I don't have enough coals to cook weeniz all aftanoon, not to mention keepin' it goin faw cawfee at night, which is how we awliss picnic at Guardid."

Non-Rler: "Coals?"

Rler: "Coals. You know. Coals. Fweeniz."

Non-Rler: "What's fweeniss?"

Rler: "Saugys. Bellybustiz. The only way to cook'em is on coals."

Non-Rler: "But what's coals?"

Rler: "Coals. Chock-o."

Non-Rler: "Chock-o?"

Rler: "What you use to cook on a bobbicue."

Non-Rler: "Oh. Barbecue. You mean charcoal. Charcoal cubes. For hot dogs."

Rler: "Right. Coals f'weeniz. And if it's not too much to hax, d'you have any umbrelleris I can bahro as well?"

Non-Rler: "Umbrellas?"

Rler: "Right. Umbrelleris. In case of vain."

Non-Rler: "Vain?"

Rler: "Uh-huh. Last time in Guardid, we got nailed by an utta downpaw."   *(Continued)*

Non-Rler: "Utta?"

Rler: "Utta. Sheea. Yuge. Enawmous."

Non-Rler: "Oh. What did you do?"

Rler: "Van all d'way to the pocking lot."

Non-Rler: "Van?"

Rler: "All d'way."

Non-Rler: "How did it end up?"

Rler: "Wou'int y'know it. It was beea-lee comin' down by the time we got to ah cahs."

Non-Rler: "Cahs?"

Rler: "Uh-huh. So we teuhned around and went back to the grills. Weea Roe Dyelindas - we don't let a lih'il vain stop a bobbicue, even though it did put the fiya out."

Non-Rler: "Fiya?"

Rler: "Fiya. In the coals."

Non-Rler: "You mean the charcoal."

Rler: "Right. The chock-o. You got any I can bah-ro?'?

D

D'BOATAYUZ: Both of you. "I run a high calliba establishment. If you can't b'have y'selves, d'boatayuz can leave the Foxy Lady right now."

D'SIDE: Resolve. What Biw Clih'in seemed to have a hard time doing early in his administration. "I just teuhned 50 and am in a mayja quandry azza Roe Dyelinda. I mostly read the Sundy paypa to look f'people I know, but at this stage of my life, I can't d'side whetha to stot wit the mavitches aw the obits."

"D' BOATAYUZ

D'WAY: The way. "I tole my brothin-lawr in Chicago - 'You shoulda been in McCoy lass night. He clobbid that ball all d'way ova the fence, halfway to P'tucket Industrial Highway. What a hitta.' He says, 'Whaddaya mean by 'D'way?' I tell him, 'I shou'int waste my time talkin' to you. You don't unnastand baseball.' "

DAWDA: Opposite of son. Also pronounced, Doorta. "I don't keea what Dahris Meuhphy lets heuh dawda do, y'not goin' to any rock concit at the Civic Senta young lady. Am I kleea? And as faw datin', y'fatha says y'not gonna be allowed to do that until he's dead."

DAWDER: Yet another pronunciation of 'Dawda' primarily used when followed by a vowel. "We just heuhd ah dawder ris feuhst in heuh class at Creanston East. She was the stah peuhfawma in the most impawtent test. She had the biggest haia."

DAZZIT: Yes m'am, that will be all. "I said, 'I'll take a vaniller frosted, an old fashioned, a Bavarian cream, a Bawston cream, a French crewla, a buttanut, a buttamilk, a honey dip, an apple & spice, a peanut butta & jelly ecleah, an apple cahmul, a strawbreeze & cream and a chawclit mocher.' The Dunkin' Donitz casheea said, 'Zattall?' I said, 'Yes, dazzall.' She said, 'You shoowa? Zattit?' I said, 'I'm shoowa. Dazzit.' "

DEARY MOTT: Not to be confused with Cum'buh'lin Fahms. "I may be only a twenny-yeea-old guy, but I'm maw than qualified to weahk the counta heah at Deary Mott. I got plenny of expeerienz dealin' wit th' public in high-powwid seuhviss jobs. Got a drawful of nametags and haia-nets to prove it."

DECKA: Description of various houses. "I tole an outtastayta th'otha day that my motha still lives in the old triple decka, and he dih'int get it. He says, 'What's a triple decka?' I says, 'You know, a tree family.' He says, 'What's a tree family?' I says, 'C'mon, double decka, triple decka; two family, tree family.' He says, 'Oh, you mean a three family house?' I tole him this is Roe Dyelin - the weuhd 'house' isn't neccessary. Around heah, 'triple decka' aw 'tree family' is good enough."

Rler: "I keeant bveak away this aftanoon afta all. I'll be speh'in the day behind my deks."

Non-Rler: "You're what?"

Rler: "My deks."

Non-Rler: "What's a deks?"

Rler: "What kind of quekshun is that to hax? Evvybody knows what a deks is."

Non-Rler: "I don't. What's a deks?"

Rler: "Weea y'do paypa weahk."

Non-Rler: "Paypa weahk?"

Rler: "Right. Paypa weahk. Y'file haffa it and troe th'otha haf in the gobbij bakset."

"What's a gobbij bakset?"

DENNISS: Extrax moluzz. "My denniss tole me he's seen bad t'bacca stains befaw, and bad tea stains, but I had the weahst cawfee milk stains he'd evva run across on a patient's teeth. Then he haxed me about the yella stains. 'Del's,' I said."

DEPOSITA: Eldlee people who gave their life's savings to creh'it union prezdints so they could buy Ferraris and condominiums in West Palm. "Honey? Joe at the orfuss. Make a rezzavation faw the Capital Grille. Weah in fat city t'night; just saw a deposita walk into the lobby."

DEVELOPIZ: Got multi-million dollar loans from Creh'it Union prezdints in return for taking them golfing. "Trust me, mea'm, you don't need my tax reteuhns f'this loan application; just put down that I golf wit

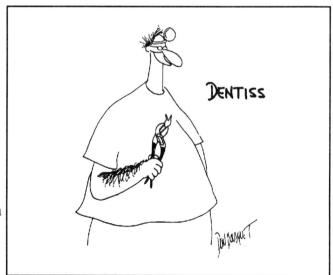

Peeta N., Joe B., and Joe M. Huh? You nuts? A'cawse I don't ack-chili plan to build condos theah; its wetlans. I'm just gonna hold it a week, flip it f'double its price and play options wit the profit. Huh? How's my buy-a gonna affawd to pay me double faw it? Wake up, honey - witta creh'it union loan.''

DISHEEA: The current year. ''Now that the Genrasemblee's passed mand'tory cah inshurnce, when ah they gonna make Roe Dyelin compeh'a'tive faw mannafatchurin? Disheea? Dream on.''

DOCK: Comes earlia in winna. ''I was in Newpawt talkin' to the new hobba-masta they just hiyud from outtastate. I said, 'I'm leavin', I don't like the dock.' He said, 'What's wrong wittit?' I said, 'What ah you talkin' about - I said I'm goin' home because I don't like the dock.' He said, 'It's the best dock in Roe Dyelin.' Fine-lee, I figyid it out and tole 'em, 'Not the boat dock - the dusk.' The problem wit Roe Dyelin is we nevva give outtastaytas enough trainin'.''

DOTS: Poppla bahroom game. ''Peuhson-lee, I'd ratha play touch football, but I heah the inshurnce investigatiz ah videotapin' people on weahkiz comp, which would ruin my case, so waddaya say we just do dots wit Mock at the bah.''

Non-Rler: "You ever been to Newport?"

Rler: "Two tree dimes."

Non-Rler: "Two-tree dimes?"

Rler: "Right. Two-tree dimes."

Non-Rler: "I didn't ask you about money. I asked if you've been to Newport."

Rler: "Two-tree dimes."

Non-Rler: "You want to talk money, we'll talk money. Have you ever lost money at Jai Alai in Newport?"

Rler: "Fidolla."

Non-Rler: "What's 'fidolla'?"

Rler: "How much I lost. Fidolla. On video poka"

Non-Rler: "Oh - video poker. I've always wondered - what kind of coins you need to play that machine?"

Rler: "Kawtiz."

Non-Rler: "What's kawtiz? I asked you about coins. What size for video poker?"

Rler: "Kawtiz. It costs faw kawtiz p'play. Aw maybe it just takes a dolla. I f'get."

Non-Rler: "I don't think you're following me. Have you ever actually been to Newport Jai Alai?"

Rler: "Two-tree dimes."

DOUGHBOY: One of tree major food groups in Roe Dyelin during the summa. Also: common reason for triple bypass. ''I promise ma, it won't ruin my suppa. Let me have one doughboy - extra sheugah-covvid - and I sweah I'll eat my whole shaw dinna az soon as I'm done wit the Free-fall Plunge.''

DOWNCELLA: In the basement. ''I tole 'em I dih'int have a guess beh'room, but he could stay downcella. He said, 'What kind a' cella?' I said, 'Downcella.' He said, 'Zat lyka wine cella?' I said, 'No, it's just downcella.' He asks: 'What's a downcella?' I tell him: the oppsit a' addick. Wheah I keep my boila. Doancha lissen?' ''

DOWNCITY: Downtown. ''Got me a room at the Biltmaw. No way I'm goin' all d'way downcity from Woonsocket and back the same day. That's almost theuhty minutes each d'rection.''

DRAW: Storage unit, usually found in beh'rooms and kitchens. ''The spatuler goes in the top draw, the cookie cuttiz in the neks one; the can opena and pot holdiz in the theuhd draw, and the turkey baysta in the fawth. As faw the nut cracka, cheese grayta, egg tima and bah'ul tops - they all go in the bah'um draw. I'll tell ya - ya want to weahk on y'Roe Dyelin axxent, the kitchen's the place.''

DRAWRIN: Popular lottery game. ''I used to only do the drawrin, but now I'm into Keno, bingo, video gambling, Las Vegas nights, video poker, scratch-off tickets, Jai Alai, the dogs, simulcast racing, Powwa Ball and the lottree. But I sure hope the Genrasemblee doesn't approve casinos in Roe Dyelin; I don't bleeve in them.''

DRAW

Decades ago, as a young adult, Alfred Glaude heard a certain expression throughout Rhode Island that he found nonsensical, but presumed was a brief fad that would fade.

Not quite. Today, Mr. Glaude's own grandchildren have begun to use the expression. He offers a typical example:

"My dad works at the Journal."

"So doesn't mine."

This, of course, is the Rhode Island way of saying, "So DOES mine."

Second example:

"My grass is real green this year."

"So isn't mine."

Mr. Glaude wonders whether he's the only one who hears such odd local language use.

I'm sorry, Mr. Glaude, I'm afraid most of us don't too.

The Rhode Island Dictionary

E

EASSIDE: When mentioned in conversation, almost always preceded by the words, 'The fashionable...' ''I don't know how the rest 'a the city stands stane up heah in the summa. It gets so beastly. What we do is close the Easside faw the season, move haffa it to Lih'il Compton so we can beach at Warn's Point, and the otha half to Neargansett so we can beach at the Dunes. I'm tellin' ya, walk down Bennfit Street in August, and you won't find a single Chip, Muffy, Tad, Missy, Kip, Buffy, Bitsy, Bif, Kiki aw Bink. And you'll know the summa's ova when you see the keah'vans of Vovo Station Wagons coming back up the two innastates.''

EAVIA: Area. ''I was thinkin' of calling the guhvanah's orfuss direckly to protest the closing of my eavia branch of the veekil rej-stree, but maybe I'll just call the tawk shows instead. If he heah's it on the eea-waves, he'll do it.''

EEA K'DISHNA: Popular brands made by Genra 'Letrick and Kerry-a. ''We usually sell 1,000 eea k'dishnas a yeea. The first tree go between Motch and July. The last 997 sell between 10 and 11 a.m. on August fawth when the temp'scha hits 101, and ev-vyone breaks down the daws in panic. That's the thing about Roe Dyelindas; they awliss plan ahead.''

Dr. Lorraine Bloomquist, now at URI, found herself confused during conversations with her new neighbor upon first moving to Rhode Island. The neighbor kept mentioning her daughter, Dahner. Or was it Donner? Either way, Dr. Bloomquist found it an odd name for a girl. At last, she asked the neighbor to spell it.

The neighbor seemed surprised that anyone wouldn't understand so simple a name. But she went ahead and spelled it anyway.

"D-o-n-n-a."

EGGSTA: Home of illih-arit woodcuttiz. ''We were so offended that a state troopa would ak-chili refeuh to all of us down heah in Eggsta as illih-arit woodcuttiz that we kahvved up his bavvicks wit chainsawrs.''

ELDLEE: Only group of Roe Dyelindas who don't speed up on yelliz. '' 'Memba those creh'it union protests? Lemme give you some advice. In Roe Dyelin, you can make the guhvanah mad, the state police mad, even the Speaka 'a the House mad. But make the eldlee mad and hoo-wee, it's ova.''

ENNIJEE: Energy. ''Y'take ennigee costs, weahka's comp, high taxes, lowa ovaseas wages & and an occasional rigid union and you got the latest Roe Dyelin riddle. Heah goes: How does a mannafack-churra make a small fawtchin in Roe Dyelin? Comes heah witta big fawtchin.''

ERVIN AH L'VENE: Brown grad now a network news economic reporter. ''Don't get me wrong, I like Dan Ratha, Peeta Jennings, Andrear Mitchell, Mawley Sayfa, Willid Scott and Diane Sawya - but no one knows numbas like Ervin Ah L'Vene. His only problem is he tawks witta funny axxent. Juss like all those newscastas do. You know - the old, 'Good evening, I'm from nowheah,' axxent. I don't know how that happened to a nice kid from P'tucket.''

Rler: "Let's hit IHOP faw breh'fuss."

Non-Rler: "Fine. I can use some strong coffee.

Rler: "Me too. Peuhsonlee, I might awda ekspresso."

Non-Rler: "You mean espresso."

Rler: "That's what I said. Ekspresso. You gonna get aigs and bacon?"

Non-Rler: "I'll pass. I don't eat eggs and bacon anymore."

Rler: "Ak-chili, so don't I."

Non-Rler: "Pardon?"

Rler: "So don't I."

Non-Rler: "I said I don't eat bacon."

Rler: "So don't I. I heah its bad faw y'otteries."

Non-Rler: "Can we get something clear. What do you mean by 'So don't I'?"

Rler: "Me neitha."

Non-Rler: "I guess that's what I thought you meant. Anyway, we've got to make this a quick bite. If I'm even five minutes late for work, my boss gives me a hard time."

Rler: "So doesn't mine."

F

FAHLLID: Followed. "I leave the Easside, drive to Green and fly all the way to Aruba to get away from it all. Then I get the most isolated hotel on the island. I mean, I cou'int have gotten fahtha from Prahvdince if I tried. My feuhst night theah, I head out the pool. I look at this couple sih'in neks to me and say, 'Wheah ah you from?' Ansa? 'Prahvdince.' Teuhns out he's a moova from Mount Pleasant, she weahks f'the state. I said - 'You fahllid us down heah, dih'int you?' He says he was thinkin' the same thing about us. Don't hax me why that happens, but no matta wheah Roe Dyelindas go on vacation, we awliss run into someone else from Roe Dyelin."

FAWSTA: Town known for canceling school even at rooma of snow. Many radio lissiniz think the town's full name is Fawsta-Glawsta. "I had it wit the deuht, grime and gahbitch in the city, so I moved up heah to Fawsta. A lot of people ah doin' that, y'know. I heah a nice young man from Johnston bought the proppity juss neks daw to me to get away from it all. Can't wait to meet him. I think 'iz name's Louis Vinagro. Know 'im?"

FAWTY DOLLIS: Cost of a week's supply of hair mousse for average Cvann-stin West coed. "I can't bleeve it - I just won a dolla-fifty in Keno. I nevva win anything. Remahkable. 'Course, I had to spend fawty dollis on tickets feuhst..."

FAYVA FACTREE: See "Genrasemblee."

FEEL GOLD: Football term. "What a game. Brown is behind Columbier by two points, but in the last figh seh'ins, they kick a feel gold from the fawty yod line. That makes them 2-8 f'the season - an incredible rekkit f'Brown. I bet they'd have haffa chance of bee'ihn Hope High this yeea."

FEVVA: Time it took to build the Jamestown Bridge. "I've got enough time to drive you to Bawston to go shoppin' f'the mawnin' and then back down to Newpawt faw a late lunch, but I'm sahree, I don't have time to take you to the Rej-stree to help you get a new license. That takes fevva."

FIDOLLA: The bill Lincoln appears on. "Fidolla? Ah you kiddin'? He'll laugh you outta 'iz orfuss. If yaw gonna bribe a may-a in this state, you need to pay at leese twice that much."

FIYABEUHD: An old Pontiac model favored by young male Roe Dyelindas. "It's time f'you to be jealous because I've got one of the last 1986 Pontiac Fiyabeuhd Trans Eams on the road. It's the shoppist machine on Route 95. Mine 'az a 5.0-leeta powwa plant witta faw-barrel cobbarayta. It's maw than a muscle cah - it's a brute. It's a beast, a fiend, a rogue and a monsta. It's a snarla, a growla, a grumbla and a rumbla. The guys in Johnston drool when I drive by. I love my cah."

FLAHRIDER: Roe Dyelin's lodgest southern suburb. In some cases pronounced Flahrida. "Just this mawnin', walking to the Seven-levin, I ran into Mahgrit, Marie-er, Ant-nee, Joe, Gregree, Peeta and Victa. Wheah else besides Flahrider can you spend the winna and still feel you're in Cvann-stin? I speshlee love shoppin' in Palm Beach. Except when ah they gonna get wittit and open an Ann in Opes on Worth Bullavod?"

FLAHRIDER

FOMMACIST: Ant-knee's job befaw he ran faw Treszhuh. "I've had sheuga f'faw yizz now but my fommacist has kept it unda control. Funny, I was outtastate once and tole a fommacist theah, 'Can y'help wit sheuga?' He said, 'This is a drug sto-wuh, ma'am. You want a groze-ree sto-wuh.' Imagine a fommacist not knowin' what sheuga is."

FRENNAMINE: A close acquaintance. "Buddy Cianci? Eeza real close frennamine. I mean, you tell me - the guy's the may-a of Prahvdince, a busy man, but he comes to my block potty evvy yeea because I ask him. Just a lih'il block potty, but like I say, he's a frennamine, so he does me favyiz. Huh? He goes to yaw block potty, too? And you doan even know 'em? What? He goes to evvy block potty in the city - even that block on Fedril Hill wit two houses on it? Oh. I see. Well, you take Bruce Sundalin - now he's a close frennamine..."

FURSDAYEA: Follows annual fireworks. "Stanly 'n me made a deal - if I agreed to drop my weuhst female Roe Dyelin habit by th'fursdayea, he'd agree to drop 'iz weuhst male habit. So weah doin' it. He's no longa doin' the Roe Dyelin slide through stop signs, and I'm no longa goin' fawty-five in the hi-speed lane on 95."

G

G'VAYVEE: Sauce. "That's th'last time I go to Texas. I went to tree restrinz and in evvy one I asked f'red g'vayvee wit my pahster. All tree dimes, the waitress says, 'What's red g'vayvee?' I tole her: 'What else? T'mayta source f'pahaster.' Don't they know anything in Texas?"

GAGGIZ: Ova-sized hot dogs. Also called 'weeniz' or 'bellybusters.' "Take it from me: if Saugys ahnt gaggiz, no weeniz ah gaggiz."

GEDADDAHEAH: Please don't bother me. "I come back to my spawts cah to find a meeda maid righ'ihn a ticket. I tell heuh please, I'm leaving right now. But she teuhns out to be a comedian - a wise ayka. She says 'I'm sahree, the meeda proves yeuh a cheeda wit yaw two-seeda.' So I looked at heuh and said, 'gedaddaheah.' But it dih'int do any good. She nailed me. Twenny-fidollis."

GENRASSEMBLEE: Elected state body reserved for membas of the Democratic potty. Pays $5 a day. Also known as the Candy Sto-wuh. "Weea all so proud of Mike. He got 'lected to the Genraseemblee from the fawth wawd by a faw p'cent mahjin. Not bad f'the owna of a taxi company. Plus, he got on the two committees he wanted most: the conflict-a-intrist commmittee and the cab-rates committee."

GLAWSTA: (See 'Fawsta.') "So I asked this fahma sellin' bluebreeze along th'road in Glawsta whetha they were local. He said, 'Nope.' So I said, 'Weea were they grown? Maine? New Yawk?' He said, 'Nope. Fawsta.'"

GO-VA: Go over. "Pleece ma. Pleece can't I go-va Judy's and have a sleepova?

Rler: "I love eatin' at New Yawk System. Heea's the menu - y'know what y'want?"

Non-Rler: "I'm not sure yet. What are you having?"

Rler: "Same thing I get heea evvy time. Two gaggiz all d'way."

Non-Rler: "Pardon?"

Rler: "Two gaggiz all d'way."

Non-Rler: "Never heard of that. I think I'll have two of these large hot dogs with everything on it."

Rler: "Great. I'll awda. 'Scuse me, ma'am, d'boata'us would like two gaggiz all d'way."

Non-Rler: "I'm sorry ma'am - my friend misunderstood. He'd like that, but I'd like two large hot dogs with everything on them."

Rler: "Right - like I said, d'boata'us want two gaggiz all d'way."   *(Continued)*

Pleece, pleece, pleece? So we can, like, lissen to P-R-O togetha? I promise we won't go to Thaya Street, and anyway, she really needs me tonight. Heuh fatha bought heuh a new cah faw heuh 17th beuhthda, and it got a ding in the daw in a pocking lot today, and like, she's so completely depressed. Pleece?''

Non-Rler: "Sorry ma'am. My friend's a wise guy. He can order for himself, but I'd like two large hot dogs with everything on them."

Waitress: "Yes suh. I'll give this to the kitchen right now. Two gaggiz all d'way faw d'boatayuz."

GOAT: Go to. ''Want me to goat the sto-wuh faw you? I'm pick'n up some clamcakes and snail salit f'suppa and I'd be glad to get an extra cottin faw you. Ak-chili, I might give you my own cottin t'mahrra. My mun-law's vizztin from Indianer, and my uhzbinn tells me she's very rigid about suppa. Likes it traditional. I'm trine to show heuh some local flayva, but I dunno - clamcakes and snail salit? I guess I shou'int hold my brett.''

GOD: Watchman. ''Ahnold's been in the god business since I don't know when. He was a hallgod in gramma school, a lifegod summiz, a pock-god f'the state afta college and now's in sales faw a s'kyeuhtee god business. He vows he'll nevva retiya. If they fawce him out at sickty-figh, he says he'll be a crossin' god 'til they carry him away.''

GRINDA: Common reason for triple bypass. ''Gimme the All-Italia Grinda pleece. Akchili, make it the Supa-Deluxe-All-Italia-Grinda. And don't leave out the Italian salami, the Provolone, the lettiss, t'maytiz and unyinz; the oil, pickles, hot relish and oregano; the peppro-nee, pro-shoot, hot peppiz and speshlee the capocollo, which if you don't know, is Italian ham. I want it on a tawpeeda roll the size of a Timbbiline weuhk boot. And make shoowa to put a little vinega on it - but not too much; I hate grindas that ah too heavily seasoned.''

GROZE-REEZ: Available at supamockit. ''I don't keah about the biopsy; keeancil it. And f'get my date in cawt; if the judge fines me, he fines me. Not to mention you can tell my boss I'm not cummin in t'day. Theah's only one thing I got t'do right now - ameejitlee - and that's get groze-reeze. And bat-reece. It's s'posed t'sno t'mahrra. Maybe tree inches. I'm histree.''

GUIDO: Local high schoolas' description of fashion style deemed opposite of prep. One need not be Italian to wear this style. ''You checked out Tad since he transfid from Moses Brown to Cranston East? He used to be totally prepped out - Topsidas, khaki pants, Oxfid sheuht, even a bow tie wit green whales on it. Now he's gone Guido. I mean, he's Gweeded out: black evvything and gold neckchain. He's even got a black strappy t-sheuht unda 'iz black leatha jacket. He looks too awrsome to bleeve.''

GUNNA: Going to. ''I weuhk azza Roe Dyelin drivin' teacha and have one basic rule. If y'gunna pull out of a pockin' lot into busy traffic, nevva inch out while waitin' faw a break in th'passin' cahs. Awlisss drive right into the feuhst travel lane - all d'way - and stay theah while evvyone sweuhves around you until they've got no choice but t'let you in. It's how evvyone does it around heah. I call it the Roe Dyelin road block.''

Rler: "Hawaiiya."

Non-Rler: "Fine. Thanks for asking."

Rler: "That's not how you respond to a 'hawaiiya' in Roe Dyelin."

Non-Rler: "How should I?"

Rler: "This way: 'Goodinyoo.' That's one weuhd. I say, 'Hawaiiya;' you say, 'Goodinyou.' Then I respond with one weuhd: 'Hangin'intheah.' "

Non-Rler: "All right. Thanks for the lesson. I've got to run. Have a nice day."

Rler: "And that's not how you say goodbye in Roe Dyelin."

Non-Rler: "How might I do that?"

Rler: "Also with one word."

Non-Rler: "And what's that word?"

Rler: " 'Avvagoodwon.' "

Non-Rler: "I'll remember."

Rler: "So th'standit greeting in Roe Dyelin goes as follas: 'Hawaiiya.' 'Goodinyoo?' 'Hanginintheah.' 'Avvagoodwon.' "

Non-Rler: "Got it."

Rler: "But if you want to have a longa conv'sation, I can brief you on that, too."

Non-Rler: "Go ahead."

Rler: "Okay, pay attention. The typical longa Roe Dyelin exchange goes like this: 'Hawaiiya?' 'Goodinyoo?' 'Hanginintheah.' 'Scone-on?' 'Nah'much.' 'Meeneitha.' 'Avvagoodwon.' 'Tawktya.' "

Non-Rler: "I missed one in there. What's 'Scone-on' mean?' "

Rler: "What's goin' on."

Non-Rler: "Got it. Thanks for the lesson. Avvagoodwon."

Rler: "Not bad faw an outtastayta."

The Rhode Island Dictionary

RIer: "I'm going to make a gvayvee.

Non-RIer: "I thought we were having spaghetti."

RIer: "We ah. That's why I'm making a gvayvee."

Non-RIer: "What do we need gravy for if we're making spaghetti?"

RIer: "Faw puh'ihn on the spaghetti."

Non-RIer: "I'd rather have it with sauce."

RIer: "Source?"

Non-RIer: "Sauce."

RIer: "That's what I'm doing. I'm making a gvayvee."

Non-RIer: "If it's not too much trouble, I'd like just sauce on mine."

RIer: "No problem. That's what I'm makin'. Gvayvee's source."

Non-RIer: "Gravy's what?"

RIer: "Source."

Non-RIer: "Let's go back to the beginning. All I want on my spaghetti is sauce."

RIer: "You'll get it. I'm makin' a gvayvee..."

Paulette Caron-Andreas married a man originally from New Jersey. Back in Rhode Island, where the two settled, she was able to prove her linguistic superiority to her husband by explaining local lexicon whenever it came up - particularly at restaurants, where he was confused by such concepts as a "grinder" being edible.

Then, while traveling once, the two ended up in Philadelpia. They sat down at a sandwhich shop. Paulette briefly forgot that not everyone talks as Rhode Islanders do and ordered a grinder. To her husband's delight, the burly man behind the counter looked at her and barked, "Youwan-nawhat?" Paulette carefully explained what a grinder was.

"Oh," the burly counterman finally said. "Lady, you want a hoagie." Across the divide of dialects, they understood each other.

Then, without thinking, she ordered a coffee cabinet...

H

HAMBEUHG: Less popula in Roe Dyelin than weeniz. "I was in Caliphonia last week, and ev-vyone kept sane 'hambeuhga' - wit an 'ah' on the end. I've nevva heuhd 'hambeugh' pro-nounced wit an 'ah' on the end befaw. Those ah weiahd people."

HAPAST FAW: Close to suppa. "Jeez, it's hapast faw. We betta leave Prahvdince right now f'Bristol and find some open sidewalk faw ah foldin' cheahs, umbrella, coola, blanket and grill. By 6 p.m. the traffic will awready be impossible faw t'mahrra's Fawth of July Parade. Real Roe Dyelindas treat that parade like buying tickets to the Soopa Bowl; smot ones get theah the night befaw."

HAVEN BROTHAS: Downcity lunch cot. "Did I heah someone say Pawdogs ah on the EPA Supafund list? They got nuthin' on us, pal. Sposelee, some advance man from the White House had a Haven Brothas hot dog f'suppa when he came to town lasheea and still tastes it when he gets up evvy mornin'. Now Al Gaw has an entiah division of the EPA wea-hking on what to do about long teuhm dis-posal of ah weeniz. They say the things have a a half life almost as long as pluto-nium-239."

HAWAIIYA?: It's so nice to see you. "Hey Ahtha. Howaiiya? Yo. Ayy. Sup? Scone'on? Nuttin? Imottaheah. Layta. Tawktya."

HAXED: Inquired. Sometimes pro-nounced, 'Ast.' "When I haxed him why he wasn't having 'iz 'Time' at the 1025, he said it wasn't big enough, so he's doing it at the Venus. At feuhst, he wasn't shoowa - he worried 'bout a Roe Dyelin politician havin' a Time outtastate. But he figyas that

> This story, with a minor adjustment or two, was sent in by Lee McGillicuddy. She may well have meant it tongue-in-cheek, but apocryphal stories sometimes hold as much truth as real ones. Here it is:
>
> A Rhode Islander arrived in Florida after a flight from Green. Upon debarking at Tampa airport, he was approached by the greeting agent.
>
> "Hawaiiya?" said the Rhode Islander.
>
> The agent replied: "No sir, y'all in Tampa."
>
> A week later, the same Rhode Islander debarked at L.A. International and ran into the same agent.
>
> "Hawaiiya?" he said again.
>
> "No sir," came the response. "But y'all are get-tin' closer."

between the the overdone chandaleahs and the soopa-deep tubs of meatballs-n'-gvayvy - not to mention lobsta Newbeuhg - theah's a little bit of Roe Dyelin right theah in Mass-chusiss.''

HAXUM: What Rhode Island male drivers refuse to do while lost, especially when their date or wife is in the cah. ''Will you please stop and haxum wheah Benny's is? I promise I won't think yaw lessava man. Honey, I know you can find it y'self, but we've been lookin' faw tree owwas now.''

HEE-WE-AH: Here we are. ''New Bed-fit's anotha reason why livin in Roe Dyelin - wheah I've been my whole life - is special. Hee-we-ah, just a half owwa from the city immawtilized in Moby Dick. Some day, I even hope to visit it. A'cawse, I teuhned 81 last month, and...''

HOD: Not easy. ''In most states, it's hod to to visit a foreign country: you half to bawd an airplane and fly ova-seas. It's a diffrint stahry in Roe Dyelin. Spend figh minutes drivin' from Atwells Avenue to Fox Point to Benefit Street and you've visited It-lee, England and Portugal. Three nations in figh minutes - not bad. Take anotha half owwa to drive to Winsocket and yaw in France, which also isn't bad. That is, if you don't mind y'host sayin', 'Throw me down the steeahs my shoes.' ''

Sandra Navratil De May was raised in Missouri, moved around the country a fair amount and finally settled in Rhode Island a few decades ago. As far as regional dialect, she knew Boston had a reputation for one, but didn't think smaller places, like Rhode Island, did. She found out soon enough.

She had five children, all under ten. One day, her oldest came home and announced he was singing "homminy" in school. That was a new one on Sandra.

Not long after, the middle child announced she was going "skay'in" at the ice rink.

Sandra also remembers visiting a local doctor's office when her youngest child was three - and had yet to pick up any of the local accent. There in the office, the little girl began to play cards.

At one point, she looked up at an elderly Rhode Island man also waiting for an appointment and said, "Pick a card."

The man seemed confused by what Sandra's daughter was saying. He looked at his wife for help, and his wife offered it: "She means pick a COD," the woman said.

Sandra herself was once corrected on how to speak properly in her new home state. She remembers asking for a Milky Way candy bar - dark chocolate.

"Oh," came the response, a bit condescendingly. "You mean DOCK chocolate."

HOLLDAY FITNISS SENTAS: Wheah Roe Dyelin women exxacise in leotods made with dental floss up the back. ''Me? I yoosta be a pleecemin in Winsocket, but I' been on comp f'figh yizz from throwing my back out, so I've taken up powwa liftin' at the Hollday Fitness Sentas instead.''

HOLLDAY: Holiday. "Waddaya mean you don't get VJ day off in Nebrasker? I thought evvybody had VJ day off. It's a mayja nashnil hollday."

HOLLY: Last American-made brand of motacycle. "Welcome to the Holly club, but rememba ah basic rule: You're not a real Roe Dyelin Holly owna if you leave its muffla on."

HOMMINY: Seen by Swamp Yankees in the outlands of Glawsta as the big city. "New Yawka stopped his cah and asked me wheah a place named 'Har-mo-nee' is. I said, 'Nevva heuhd of it.' He said, 'It's right heah in the map - Har-mo-nee.' I said I've lived in Glawsta my whole life and nevva heuhd of it. Lemme see that map.' So he showed me. I said, 'Oh - you mean 'Homminy.' Shoowa. Why dintcha call it that? We like to pvonounce ah weuhds proplee heah in Glawsta."

HOT ATTACK: What one 'takes' if one eats too many Grindas. "I cou'int bleeve it, Mahgrit - it was akchili him. Ahnold Shwottsnegga. At Gold's Gym. I went theah to do step aerobics and check out th' guys when all of a sudden Ahnold walks in on some publicity toowa, and Mahgrit - onnis-t'- God - he stots flexin' 'iz ahms. I jussta 'bout took a hot attack. My ticka juss stopped cold.' "

HOT: Valentine. "Chevul busted my hot right in two. Dumped me f'Vinnie. And I'm convinced I know why: he has betta weight-trainin' equipment downcella than I do."

Kathleen Elion, a born Ocean Stater, concedes she had a pretty extreme Rhode Island accent growing up. Then, in 1975, she moved with her husband to Wisconsin. It took five years of living there for it to happen, but at last, she began to lose her old dialect.

In time, when she would hear the old accent from others, she realized how, well, different Rhode Islanders sound. So a part of her was relieved to have left her original way of speaking behind.

In 1980, the family moved again, this time down south, first to North Carolina and then Kentucky. Now a southern accent began to seep into her family. But she barely realized how deep the new accent was getting until one day when her youngest child ran into the house crying because she'd fallen and hit her head.

As Kathleen tells it, the child didn't pronounce head as 'head.' She pronounced it as 'heeaaaadddd.'

"Four syllables," recalls Kathleen. That's when she realized it was time to come back to Rhode Island.

The family's been back several years now. Kathleen realized she was truly home when she mentioned to a friend that she needed to go shopping for a new winter parka.

Only she didn't pronounce it parka.

It came out "pocker."

But somewhere deep, it felt good to be a Rhode Islander again.

RIer: "I'm psyched. I'm leaving on my hollday next week."

Non-RIer: "There's no holiday next week."

RIer: "There is for me. I'm going to Na'amsha. I've been lookin' fawwid to this hollday f'munts."

Non-RIer: "I still don't get it. There's no holiday next week. Do you mean vacation?"

RIer: "Don't get technical. Hollday, vacation - what's the diffrence?"

Non-RIer: "A holiday's not the same thing as a vacation where I come from."

RIer: "It is in Roe Dyelin. Anyway, I'm headin' to the mall to get ready faw it. The stowuhs theah have everything on special."

Non-RIer: "On special?"

RIer: "Right. Half-price."

Non-RIer: "You mean 'On sale.' "

RIer: "On special, on sale - what's the difference?"

Non-RIer: " 'On special' isn't the same as 'on sale' in most places."

RIer: "It is in Roe Dyelin. I'll tell you, it'll be a relief to get outta my triple decka."

Non-RIer: "Your what?"

RIer: "My triple decka. My tree-family."

Non-RIer: "Are you talking about a building with three apartments?"

RIer: "Tree apottments, triple-decka, tree-family - what's the difference?"

Non-RIer: "There's a difference in most places."

RIer: "Not in Roe Dyelin. I also have to hit the cleansas."

Non-RIer: "You mean the cleaners?"

RIer: "Same difference. Then I gotta go up th'house."

Non-RIer: "Up to what house?"

RIer: "Up th'house. Go home. Ahnt those the same thing?"

Non-RIer: "I'm afraid not in most places."

RIer: "I see. Hey. Waddaya say we go to cawfee."

Non-RIer: "What's that?"

RIer: "Go to cawfee. What else could it be?"   *(Continued)*

The Rhode Island Dictionary

Non-Rler: "You mean take a break? My friend, in most places..."

Rler: "I know what chigonna say."

Non-Rler: "Well, I can't take a break now, but salutations."

Rler: "Pleece?"

Non-Rler: "Please what?"

Rler: "Pleece nothing. 'Pleece' means 'pahdden me' in Roe Dyelin."

Non-Rler: "It does?"

Rler: "It does. Tell you what, maybe I'll have you ova to my triple decka afta my hollday, we'll go to cawfee and see whose got what on special."

Non-Rler: "You're trying to exasperate me now, aren't you?"

Rler: "Pleece?"

Elizabeth Norfrey is the Minister of Music at the Evangelical Covenant Church of Riverside. To add refinement to the choral sound, she strives to teach her singers to tone down their "r's," particularly in words like "honor" and "worship." But not in the classic Rhode Island way of turning an "r" into an "ah." Her goal is to teach a more genteel European "r" sound. It wasn't easy.

First she sought to have her singers affect "r's" the way Germans pronounce "o's." When that didn't work, she tried urging them to pronounce "r's" somewhat as the British do. That didn't work either.

At last, she had an idea. "I suggested that the vowel sound in the French word for 'I' - 'je' - would be close," she recalls. One of her male tenors, who refers to his wife as 'Linder', immediately brightened and said no problem - he knew how the French pronounce 'I.' Elizabeth told him to give it a try so the rest of the class could hear.

"Jer," he said.

I

I-NIN: The act of using an ion. "Davit youssta be suhtcha slob. Sheuht-tail awliss hangin' out, grease-stains on 'iz tie, evvything rumpled. Then he got this new job, bought me a top-a-the-line ion, and evvy day now, I'm i-nin this, I'm i-nin that. Ion my pants, he says - ion my jackit, ion my sheuht, ion my socks. Yesstay he goes nuts because I left a crinkle on his stripe. His stripe! I'm tellin' ya, Eunice, I wish they'd nevva hi-yud him azza Statie."

IDEAR: Always a dangerous sign when someone at the Genra Semblee announces they have one. "I'd luvvta go to the cawna sto-wuh off Weyborsett, but I can't. My speech teacha, Linder - who's from Tacomer and is helping a lot of kids at Ponergansett - is comin' ova in figh minutes to help me weahk on the way I move the letta 'ah' to wheah it doesn't belong. She's got Polish background, by the way, and says if I bveak the habit, she's going to rent the State House rotunder - wheah they make lawrs - teach all heuh students to dance the poker, then have a picnic aftaweuhd in Guardid Pock, and maybe take us to Cape Card. And who keahs if it rains, we'll just bring ah umbrelleris. Does she have great idears awwutt? So I can't go. But couldja pick me up some pizzer, parpcawn, tuner, bah'uld warta and soders faw d'boata'us while we weahk on the sofer? And maybe some bannaners."

IDER & LINDER: Friends named Ida and Linda. "Me 'n Ider ah speh'in the summa workin' on ah tans. We been hittin' a diffrent beach each day. We stotted at Miskwammerkit in Wes'tuhly, then Kwonn'ch'taug, Chahz-tin and Rahja Weela. She likes Roy Cahpintiz, and we both like Neahganssit, Gaurdid in Wawwick and Hawseneck in Fall Rivva. But a'cawse Skahbruh's my main favrit cuz of the guys; we like to go down theah on hot days and show off ah big, yuge...haia. Drives Roe Dyelin guys nuts."

ILL: It will. "A reffrendum to raise legislatas' pay from $5 a day to $7.50? Theah feuhst raise since the Civil Waw? The kind of compensation even prizznizz at the ACI ah entigh'uld to? Mock my weuhds - ill nevva win."

ILLINOISE: Lodge midwestin state. "I cou'int be happia, Melinder. My dawda's marrying a nice young loy-a from Illinoise. You know Illinoise - between Indianer and Iower. But it breaks my hot that she'll be moving away from Winsocket. I don't know how often we'll be geh'ihn' t'getha wit them in the fewtcha. Once a yeea? Maybe twice? I just don't know, Melinder. Theah buyin' a house in Wawwick.''

IMOTTA HEAH. Forgive me, but I intend to depart. ''Excuse me suh, but can you point me to the Steppingstone Ranch? Waddaya mean y'nevva heuhd of it? The newspaypa says it's right heah in Usquepaug. You know, home of the Roe Dyelin Cajun-Bluegrass Festival. Huh? Oh - that's in Escoheag? Hmm, Usquepaug-Escoheag - I guess I got 'em mixed up. Huh? No, I don't want Jonnycake mix now that I'm in Usquepaug. I want music. Immota heah.''

INFEEREE-AWTEE: Unworthiness. ''You'd have an infeeree-awtee complex too if evvyone thought yaw state was a subeuhbin island off New Yawk city.''

INNEE: Isn't he. ''Evvyone makes fun of Ralph aRusso faw adding an 'A' to the stot of his name. Well, laugh it up if y'want, but he's may-a f'life, innee? That's why I stay up at night repee'ihn it again and again so I get used to it: 'aCianci, aCianci, aCianci...' ''

INNIT?: Rhetorical question. ''Funny the way Roe Dyelindas still call it the Red Bridge to East Prahvdince even though they replaced it fawty yizz ago - innit? It's weiahd how some of us can't let go of the past. See ya layta. Got to make a deposit at the Industrial National Bank.''

ION'NEE: Irony. ''Heah's an ion'nee faw ya. Colonial Roe Dyelindas beuhn down an entiya British tax ship - the Gaspee - and we get almost no publicity faw it. In Boston, they tro a lih'il bit of measly tea in the hobba, and they end up makin' all the histree books. I guess the Boston patriots had betta pea-ah people than ah Roe Dyelin patriots.''

Mike Barnacle, a businessmanand Rhode Island transplant, walked out of the delivery room at Women and Infant's Hospital. He had just had his first child - a boy. He and his wife Sally decided to name it "Ian." Now the delivery nurse asked Mike to follow her while she took the infant to be weighed. As he walked into the hallway, a second nurse that had helped with the labor earlier stepped out of the elevator.

"Oh," she said. "You had the baby awready." Mike didn't really notice at the time, but she had a strong Rhode Island accent. "What's his name?" the nurse asked.

"Ian," said Mike.

"Oh," said the nurse. "I thought it was supposed to be a boy."

"It is," said Mike. "We did have a boy."

The nurse looked puzzled. "But you named it Ian," she said.

Now Mike was puzzled. "Yes," he said. "We named him Ian."

"You named a boy Ian?" she said.

Then Mike realized what she was thinking. "Ian," he said. "I-A-N.

"Oh," she said. "I thought you were saying Ann. A-N-N."

The Rhode Island Dictionary

IT-LEE: European country somewhere south of Austree-er and west of Albaynee-er. ''I'm de-clea'in' my canditzy f'the Roe Dyelin state senate today. And though my name's John Gilgun, you gotta bleeve me: my motha's from Itlee, my uncle's from Itlee, my eeant's from Itlee, my grandfatha's from Itlee. Basically, I'm Italian. A'cawse, if you happen to be an Irish voter, my fatha's from Dublin, my uncle's from Galway, my grandfatha's from Lim-rick, my grand-motha's from Cawk...''

J

J'PEEAN: One of few countries where Cong. Jack Reed can buy suits off the rack. ''I opened a drive-thru Roe-Dyelin-Doughboy-&-Cawfee-Milk-Hut in J'peean two munts ago and haven't gotten a single customa. I'm thinkin' of complainin' to the U.S. Depottmint of Commiss. The only explanation I can think of is some kinda hidden unfeah trade barry-iz. I mean, what else could it be?''

JEET: A question among co-workers at lunchtime. Roughly: Have you eaten yet? Long form is 'Jeejet?' ''Jeet? Me neetha. Waddaya say we head down t'Sow Kingstin and get hot dogs from those girls who sell'em in bikinis at that roadside stand? If that's too fah, we'll just hit a Sub Shop. Ready? Sco.''

JEFFISON: Got all credit for renouncing the crown even though Roe Dyelin did it feuhst. ''It's on Jeffison Bollivod. In what city? What kind of question is that? Ev-vyone knows wheah Jeffison Bollivod is. No one in the histree of Roe Dyelin has evva said, 'Jeffison Bollivod in Wawwick.' It's just, 'Jeffison Bollivod.' Kind of like Minra Spring Avenue. If you don't know what town Jeffison Bollivod aw Minra Spring Avenue's in, you don't have a right to go theah.''

JOOL-A-REE: State's biggest industry. ''Nicest Jool-a-ree I evva sawr. Byoo-tee-ful gold neckchains, gold bracelets, rings on almost evvy finga. Dawthee, he stood out maw than almost any man at Skahbruh Beach.''

JOONYA: Reputed to still be a mayja fawce in awganized crime. ''C'mon, admit it. Deep down, yaw disappointed that Bawston's become maw the centa of the New England mob than Roe Dyelin; that you wish Joonya was half the man his fatha was; that even though it was the mob, you were proud deep down that this was one indistree we weuh betta rat than Bawston. Admit it.''

JOOZEET: Asking more than one person whether they've eaten. Often followed by the response, 'Squeet,' which is the compressed form of 'Let's go eat.' ''Joozeet? Yin th'mood faw pizzer? What'll it be? Pizzer Hut? Little Seeza's? Caseuhta's, Domino's, Mineuhvas, Uncle Tony's, Papa Gino's, Ronzio's aw Uno? Y'not in the mood? How about Chinese. What'll it be? The Chine-er Inn? Chine-er Palace? Lil Chopstix? Chine-er Goddin, Chine-er Pearl, Chine-er Sea, Chine-er Stah, the Mandrin Texaco...Huh? Not in the mood? You just want a grinda rat the dye-na? Me too. Squeet.''

JUPIDAH: Lodgest planet. ''Feuhst y'got Meuhcuree, then Venus, then Eauhth. Afta that y'got Mahz, follid by Jupidah, Satin, Uraniss, Neptune and Pluto. If y'keep goin' past the Solah System, you'll hit the Big Dippah, the Lih'il Dippah, and all the stahs and stah clustas of the univeuhse, many of which were ideh-afied by Copeuhnicus. I'll tell ya, if y'wanna give a Roe Dyelin accent a good weahkout, theah's nuthin' like 'stronomy.

JWANNA: Do you want to? Also - Would you like?: ''Jwanna cawfee? How about a cawfee milk? No? A Del's? Jwanna an ice cawfee then? No again? C'mon, I'm theuhsty - y'gotta be in the mood to drink something? Jwanna a cawfee cabinet? An orful-orful? I got it - an ekspresso. No? All right. One more idear. I rememba a place wheah we can still get an old Roe Dyelin soder fountain drink most people have f'got. Name: Lime Rickies. Jwanna have one a' those? A Lime Ricky? Great. Sco.''

For those who might think the more extreme bits of Rhode Island jargon are new, let Gregory Zeitlin set that aside. Back in 1947, he travelled the country with a musical band - all Rhode Islanders like himself - following what was then called the "Kerosene Circuit." It was called that, Gregory explains, because those were the days when parts of rural Iowa, Nebraska, Kansas and the Dakotas had no public electricity.

Mostly, Gregory's band focused on two things - playing and eating. To this day, he remembers the standard conversation exchanged among the band members at noon, the time many musicians who work late start their day. Gregory relates it in full:

"Hey man, djeetjet?"

"No. Dju?"

"No. Squeet."

Translation: 'Have you eaten yet?' 'No, have you?' 'No - let's go eat.'

But the jargon has gotten even more compressed since then. Robert Mancini was recently with a few fellow Rhode Islanders visiting a friend in Florida. The group was together talking when the Florida friend began laughing at what Mancini had just said to the other Rhode Islanders in the room. It was a question about whether the others had eaten, but not even as long a question as Gregory Zeitlin's "Djeetjet?" of 45 years ago. In Mancini's case, as in many cases in the 1990s, it comes out simply as, "Jeet?"

K

KAHVENTREE: Sometimes pronounced Carventry. Ceded to Roe Dyelin by legislatiz in Hart-
fid to seuhve as buffa between Connecticut
and West Wawwick. ''She tried to tell me
she was a real Roe Dyelinda to get in good
wit my pearints who live on Nooseneck
Road, but I found out she was a fraud
when she pvnounced it Kuhventree. Any
real Roe Dyelina weuhth his salt
pvnounces it Kahventree.''

KAWTA: Won't buy a cup of cawfee
milk these days. ''What I love about Miskwammerkit is if you got a few kawta's,
you k'navv the time of y'life wittout even
geh'in wet. They got removable tattoos, a
fearis wheel, a keeasell, a warta slide and
these awrsome soov'neah shops, which sell evvything. Like plastic lobsta claw hahmonikers,
Roe Dyelin Red back scratchas - I mean awrsome stuff.''

KIH-INS: Cute creatures that, lamentably,
grow into cats. ''I'm tellin' ya, d'boata'us
was crazy in love - engaged and evvything,
invitations mailed - but it fell apott last
weekend. Paula's got this kih-in she a-daws
named Mimi, right? Me, I have Rex the
Doabamin. So I tell heuh when we move in,
Rex will love Mimi. Then I say: 'He'll love
heuh on a Ritz Cracka.' I meant it funny,
but she tells me no way heuh kih-in's evva
movin' in wit my Doabamin. Aw she wit
me, f'that matta. It's off. She won't even
reteuhn my calls. So y'know any single

geuhls? I'm back in the mockit. Long as they don't own kih-ins.''

KO-HOG. Quahog. As close to an official state animal as exists in Roe Dyelin. ''Ah famlee lives f'the Wickfit Ko-hog festival. We don't eat f'two days befaw it so we can try evvything: lobstas, lih'il-necks, clamcakes and steamiz. Feuhst we go right to the Stuffie Tent - nuthin' like stuffies, 'speshlee wit Portuguese sorsage. We try to be the feust to sample the winnas of the stuffie cook-off. Lasheea, my dawda Rhonder h'self won best baked-stuffed. Heuh fiancee Tony won the Ko-hog-shucking contest. That's how she met him, and they've been seein' eachotha evva since. People say

KO-HOG

theah the ultimate Roe Dyelin couple - she makes the best stuffies, and he's the state's fastest Ko-hog shucka. A peuhfick match.''

KUHBBID: Old Mother Hubbard's were bare. ''My kuhbid? Crackiz, pvetzels, pahster, salit dressin', peanut butta, kvanbevvy juice, tuner, seavvup, parpcawn, melber toast, sheuga, Cape Card bah'day'da chips, Cheevios, moshmellos, possly leaves, Veeties see-vee-ul, Kvisco, and fine-lee, sweet & sowwa source. And unfawtunately, one maw thing: cocka-roaches. Don't hax me why we Roe Dyelindas call them cockaroaches but we do.''

KUPPLA: Two meanings. (1) A few. (2) Cables used to stot a dead cah battree. ''A kuppla'us was drivin' from Kahventree all d'way t'Rocky Point. Lucklee, it being so fah, we brought two cahs. Thank God, because one broke down at Harxie Faw Corniz. But we had kuppliz to get it goin' again. Only we took it azza sign, bagged Rocky Point and went back home wheah it's safe.''

Linda Vande Vrede - maiden name 'Bessette' - is a displaced Rhode Islander now living in Phoenix. But she thinks of home often and will always remember the time she was waiting in a Rhode Island convenience store to buy milk when a man dashed in and breathlessly told the clerk that he had left his "khakis" in the store. He wondered if anyone had found them.

As Linda tells it, after looking in vain for a pair of tan pants, the clerk - as well as the rest of those in the store - suddenly realized what the man was talking about. The story had a happy ending.

His car keys were waiting on the counter, right where he had left them.

L

LASHEEA: The 12 months preceding January. "Lasheea was definitely not a good one f'business. I moved from Roe Dyelin to Caliphonia to go big-time, but it was a disasta. Feuhst, my line of kissin' dolphin earrings bombed. So did my live shrimp on a necklace. My mood rings bombed; so did my nugget watches and ankle bracelets. Then I went big into Cubic Zircony-er headlight necklaces, but they went nowheah. Next I went ba-bing, ba-bing from Jade buttaflies to Zodiac bracelits to pendants that chime. But they dih'int move eitha. I even tried pendants that hold you-know-what f'safe sex; I called it the C-locket. But nada. So I went crazy wit plating: gold plated aycawns, silva-plated sand dollis, gold-plated pine cones. Nuthin' moved. So I came home to Roe Dyelin to lick my wounds, but you know what - the phone stots ringin'. Evvy distributa in the state says this is the peufick mockit for what I've got. So hey, maybe dissheea will be betta than lasheea."

LAWR: The one product besides sausages that you don't want to watch being made in Roe Dyelin. "Personlee, as a legislata, I thought a lawr askin' creh'it unions t'get fedril inshurnce was a good idear. I nevva quite trusted RISDIC, and this lawr would've shut it down. But then the RISDIC people - nice people it teuhns out - they took me and th'otha guys from the assemblee to this fancy club on Atwells and tole us the lawr is NG. I still held my ground, but then they bawt us this great dinna - roasted peppiz, veal and cannoli f'dezeuht. So I said, hey - a nice dinna - that's as good a reason as any to vote th'way they tell me. So we nixed the bill. Neks thing I know, we gotta bankin' crisis. Now evvyone's blamin' the Generasemblee but hey, I dih'int shut the banks. Bruce did."

> **R**ler: "I doan like my pizzer."
>
> Non-Rler: "Well, I certainly like my hot dog and doughboy."
>
> Rler: "Kighvapeece?"
>
> Non-Rler: "Is that Russian? If you have something to say, say it in English."
>
> Rler: "I did. Kighvapeece?"
>
> Non-Rler: "Will you quit with the Russian already?"
>
> Rler: "Y'got plenny theah f'd'boata-us."
>
> Non-Rler: "What language is 'D'boata-us?' German?"
>
> Rler: "Pleece. I'm stovvin."
>
> Non-Rler: "I'm impressed. Is that Dutch now?"

LAYTA: Roe Dyelin for 'goodbye.' "This guy Chip comes up to me and Rhonder at Shootiz last Saddy night. He's like so Easside and prepped out you wou'int bleeve it. Sweata ovva his shoulda, blue blayza, Lacoste sheuht and Weejuns. F'the neks two owwas, he's like, 'Moses Brown this,' and 'Weela School that.' Then he stots tellin' us how his ancesstas came ovva on the Mayflowa and when did ah ancestas come ovva? I'm like, 'W'lucky they let them into Ellis Island.' Neks he stots in about how hod it is f'him to relate to anyone who dih'int go to prep school and an Ivy. That's when me and Rhonder said, 'Nice meetin ya, Chip. Avvagoodwon. Layta.'"

LES: Let us. "Heah's the plan. We drive to Texas in my uhzbin's trackta-traila, we wait until nightfaw, we sneak into the zoo compoun', we open the bon daw, we rush Fanny into the truck and drive heuh back to P'tucket. It may be illegal, but I'm sahree, Roe Dyelin no longa feels like home to me wittout that elephant in Slayda Pock. Les go."

At times, while writing this book, I've worried that I've at times exaggerated the way Rhode Islanders talk. Of course, the local accent varies in extremity, but routinely, most of us do hear vivid examples, and I got many letters describing dialect even more excessive than most I'm using here.

One example came from Mary Heaney of Warwick, a former English teacher. She included what she said was close to a verbatim account of a conversation she once had with a student in her classroom. Some of her "Roe Dyelin" spellings are a bit different from the ones I've used, but for accuracy, I'll print her account letter-for-letter:

"Yestiddee I seen you and yuh huzbin at Linkin Mawl. Didjoo see me? Yooze wuz in front of Jawdin Mosh. Is he cummin to class t'night? I wish I could of spoke witchooze, but it wuz too cole dowt, an I wuz mad at my muthuh becuz she sole my vee-cee-ah rat huh yodsale, an I almost had a hottattack. I gut a noo one, but I ain't yoostavit yet, so I cou'int tape L.A. Lore."

LOANA: Cah. "Trust me - they give the best seuhviss of any deala in the state. They even give you a loana evvy time you drop y'cah off to get the odometta teuhned back."

LOBSTA: Unofficial state crustaceon. "I was in Louisianer vizztin' my cousin Alphonse, who'd nevva been to New Englin befaw. I tole him he's got to come and have lobsta. He says, 'What's a lobsta look like anyway?' I tole him, 'Like a crawdad, but bigga.' He asks, 'Ah they easy to cook?' I tole him, 'Piece a cake. Y'talking to the Dean, the Wizzid, the original Bakemasta. Feuhst, you dig an eight-inch deep pit and line it wit rocks. Then you put wood inside and beuhn it faw tree owwas. You rake that out and fill it up wit six inches of seaweed you've wheelbarrid up from the beach. Afta that, you add yams, bah-day-diz, sorsage, carritz, crabs, hot dawgs, unyinz, periwinkles, cawn, and a'cawse, lobstas. Y'also add steemiz and mussels, but only afta you've soaked 'em good to git ridda the sand. Then you get it steamin' real good and covva it witta top - a canvass top - faw about two owwas. Bingo - y'got y'lobstas.' Like I said, piece a' cake.''

LODGE: Ovasize. ''No way I'm geh'ihn into the Roe Dyelin School of Cosmetology wittout doing something special. I mean, the competition is tougha than geh'in into Brown. But I've got it figyud out. I go to the interview not just wit big haia, but lodge haia. I mean yuge haia - massive haia, enawmiss haia. That'll prove I know my fewtcha clients.''

LOU-TEH'IT GUHVANAH: Main function is to call guhvanah's orfuss each morning to ask if he's died yet. ''I'm so proud of Vichit. The Pawsox just named him numba one relief pitcha. That means he gets to spend the rest of the season sih'ihn' on the bench wishin' he was on the mound. Mock my weuhds, he'll make a great lou-teh'it guhvanah some day.''

LOY-A

LOY-A: What one becomes after attending Suffolk night school. ''I hate to move outta state, but it's an awffa I can't refuse. A guy who runs some retail sto-wuhs down in New Yawk sawr the TV ads I produced faw a Roe Dyelin loy-a, and he says I'm peuhfect faw his oppavation. Evva heuhd of him? Calls himself Crazy Eddie.''

The Rhode Island Dictionary

M

MAH-KETTE: Ex Woonsocket Bank. Forma candy sto-wuh for developas. "You want to build condos even though you've nevva built anything but bookshelves befaw? And y'expectin' theah's someone out theah gullible enough to front you a $20 million loan? No problem. Go to Mah-kette. Wait a minute - I f'got. They shut it down. Can't imagine faw the life a' me why they'd shut down such a nice oppavation, but y'otta luck."

MAHZ: Wheah 80 percent of Roe Dyelindas thought Joe Mollicone was hiding during his absence. "They say most creh'it union officials had to be on Mahz when they approved those loans. If that's true, the creh'it union prezdints weuh on Jupidah, RISDIC was on Neptune and the Genrasemblee, which created the whole thing, was on Pluto."

MAVITCH: A dozen take place at the Venus de Milo each weekend. "He's a kohogga. She's a cosmetologist. I can't imagine a maw peuhfect Roe Dyelin mavitch. The only problem is she grew up in Cvann-stin and he's from Nawt Kingston; it's hod on the famlees to see theah kids mavvy outtatowniz."

MAWCGIDGE: What you need to afford a low numba plate in Roe Dyelin. "Peuhsonlee, I wanna be a creh'it union prezdint when I grow up. If you get behind on y'mawcgidge, you just pay it off wit money from y'best friends' accounts, tell th'audatiz it's a legal loan y'keepin' track of in y'head, and if they press you f'details, y'offa'em a muffin."

MAY-A: Vincent A. Cianci Jr.'s office for life. "Becomin' may-a is an impaw'int careea move in Roe Dyelin politics. Bein' may-a of Wawwick is a steppin' stone to the U.S. House, bein' may-a of Cvann-stin is a steppin' stone to the State House; bein' may-a of P'tucket is a steppin' stone to the big house..."

MEH'RILL STRIP: Famous actress. "Meh'rill Strip? I adawwed heuh opposih Robba Rehfeh in 'Outta Africker'. But I dint love heuh opposih Dustin Horfman in Krayma veahsis Krayma. Still, she's a big enough stah that I wou'int be s'prised if they asked heuh to do a guest spot on 'Roseanne.' "

MEMBA?: Do you by chance remember? "Doncha memba? The state animal's a red roosta, not a blue bug. Just like the state drink's cawfee milk, not Del's. The state game? That's a hod one. Keno?"

MIH-INS: Warma than gloves. "Doan f'get y'scoff, long undaweah, teuhtilneck, snow pants, neck gayta, rag socks, hat wit face mask, down mih-ins, Timbbiline boots, and chemical pak hand warmas. John Guee-awsee says it'll be a balmy fawty degrees, but I saw a flake of snow, and this is Roe Dyelin, so you haffta be ready f'anything."

Mary Kehoe devoloped a solid Rhode Island accent growing up here, then went on to graduate school at the University of Maryland where she became a teaching assistant, taking on four freshman classes in U.S. history. On her first day, she was explaining to one class about her grading system, specifically about how each mark would fit into the final grade. As she spoke, she noticed a hand go up. A student with a puzzled expression said he had a question. Mary told him to go ahead.

He did - asking if Mary would explain just what a "mock" was.

It wasn't the only time outsiders were thrown by her accent. When she moved to Indiana after marrying, her husband John would routinely offer to translate when she spoke around friends there.

Of course, that was all in good humor, but on occasion, she was asked a surprising question in what seemed to be seriousness: What was the origin of her "foreign accent?"

MOTA VEE'KIL REJ-STREE: Staffed by clerks trained at the Moscow institute of public service. "Hello, Mota Veek'kil Rej-stree inf'mation, may I help you? A new license? Easy, just walk into the building and if people ah in y'way, pass them on the right. If they won't move, make rude hand gestjas while walking down the hallway until you come to the sign that says, 'Wait Heah.' Ameetjitlee, slide right through it. Afta that, fake right and teuhn left. If anyone tries to walk by you, speed up and block them. Only yield if y'see the whites of theah eyes. Fine-lee, when you pose faw y'pitcha, do y'best t'look like a drug deala. Thank you f'calling."

MUNLAW: Mother-in-law. "I'm furious at the state. My munlaw lives in Jamestown and faw the last ten yeeas has only been vizztin' us in Wickfit once evvy six munts. She wou'int go ova that bridge. Faw me - peuhfick. Then they built a new bridge and now she visits evvy week. I'm thinkin' of movin' to Newpawt. It's technickly close-a, but no way she'll pay the toll unless she has too."

MUNTS: Twelve of them make a year. "I tole 'em 'No problem - it'll take a munt maximum.' He said, 'One munt? It'll take 50 munts at least.' I said 'Fifty? F'the state to build a little bridge ova a little faw-foot wide stream in Cum-buh-lin so they can extend a little country road? I'm tellin you - it'll take less than a munt - maybe a week.' He juss smiled, shook his head and said, 'You doan no Roe Dyelin.' ''

MUSKEETIZ: Almost as annoying as Gypsy Moths. ''I yoosta go to Breh'ihn State Pock in Newpawt but I got tie-it of the muskeetiz. Same wit Coat Pock in Bristol and Guardid in Wawwick. I spent a few summiz canoeing in the Gvate Swarmp in Sow Kingston, but the muskeetiz got to me theah, too. They even got to me in Rahja Williams in Prahvdince and Slayda in P'tucket. And a'cawse the beaches have theah sheah of muskeetiz. So mostly I go to the dogs in Lincoln. That still counts as reckveation, doesn't it?''

MUSTABIN: Must have been. ''A great guy. He gave me what mustabin the best div-vections I've evva received azza Roe Dyelinda. No street names at all; just land-mocks. He tole me to take a right past the loyiz orfuss wit the Mickey Mouse sign in the winda, then look faw the theuhd house on the left past wheah the Industrial Bank branch used to be befaw they made it into a video staw that went out of business. It was like, ba-bing, ba-bing; I dih'int miss a shot.''

MUSTIT: Grey Poupon. ''Weeniz awliss taste betta witta P'tucket Red Sox game in front of 'em. But even that won't help if you don't have any mustit. A'cawse, this being Roe Dyelin, you also need spicy meat sauce, chopped onions, plenny of cehrry sawt...''

Nancy Holst of Warwick tells this story about an out-of-state tourist who pulled his car to a halt alongside an elderly South County Swamp Yankee.

"How do you get to that beach with an Indian name?" the tourist asked.

The Swamp Yankee began his answer: "Mis-quamicutWeekapaugQuonochontaugMa-tunuck...?"

Irritated, the tourist cut him off and turned to his passenger. "Oh hell, he doesn't speak English."

Then he sped off in a jack-rabbit getaway.

Non-RI mother, recently transplanted: "Are you coming to the mall with me or not today, young man?"

Her son, already speaking Rhode Islandese: "Mizewell."

Mother: "What did you say to me, young man?"

Child: "Mizewell."

Mother: "And just what is 'mizewell' supposed to mean?"

Child: "You asked if I was comin' so I anssid."

Mother: "I expect a proper answer out of you, not a smart remark I don't understand."

Child: "It's not a smot remock. I'll go, I'll go, okay?"

Mother; "That's better. We'll leave exactly a half hour from now. All right?"

Child: "Mizewell."

The Rhode Island Dictionary

N

N'YAWK: One of many reasons for ah inferiority complex. ''He haxed me wheah I come from and I tole 'em 'Roe Dyelin.' He looked at me a lih'il funny so I said it again: 'I come from Roe Dyelin.' Fine-lee, he says, 'What paht of N'Yawk is that, anyway?' I just gave up and gave 'em the ansa he wanted: 'You know, that long thin island leading to the Hamptons.' ''

N-G: Description, usually shared between female friends, of any ex-husband or boyfriend in disfava. ''Tawk about N-G; two weeks afta he proposed to Chevul, she sawr him at Shootiz wit Rhonder. When Chevul confra'ihd him, he said Rhonder was just a nayba he was escawting to the Hot Bod contest because she lost heuh ride. But Chevul's smot enough to know that the only hot bod contest Rhonder could win is at the Slayda Pock Zoo, so she dih'int buy it. N-G is what he is.''

NA'AMSHA: About 80 miles north of Rhode Island. ''Buy a mountain home in Na'amsha? I know you had y'hot set on that when we got mavvied, Chollie, but that's tree owwas from Prahvdince. Theah's no way I'd drive that fah on weekends now that we have kids. You wanna mountain home, we'll buy something on Jerimoth Hill in Fawsta. It's ovva 800 feet - awmost as high as the Johnston landfill. What maw d'ya want?''

NAWT PRAHVDINCE: A city formed for the sole purpose of providing a place for Sal Mancini to be may-a of. ''How do I feel about Sal Mancini? Strikes me he runs a machine. Faw my taste, he's been investigay'ihd once too often. I'm not sure I trust him. He does things the old way in a new age. It's long since been time faw a change. And people have begun to wonda about Nawt Prahvdince because of him. That's my opinion. So who am I gonna vote faw faw may-a? Sal Mancini a'cawse.''

NAWT SMIFFEEL: Gateway to Uxbridge. ''Who tole you Nawt Smiffeel is to Winsocket what Nawt Prahvdince is to Prahvidence? Theah's a big difference. Nawt Smiffeel is Woonsocket's Easside, not it's nawt side - kind of like what Nawt Dottmit is to Faw Rivva. And don't f'get it.''

NEVVAMINE F'get abow'it. ''I drove a hod boggin. Feuhst he comes down to $50,000. I just shrugged, kinda yawned, and said, 'Nevvamine. Weea too fah apott to even tawk.' He said 'Wait, I'll take $45,000, but no lowa.' I said, 'No hod feelings, but nevvamine. Y'obviously don't want to sell.' That did it. He said, 'Okay, okay. I'll give you y'price. $35,000.' Do I know how to deal awwutt? I stole the thing. A two-numba Roe Dyelin license plate f'only $35,000. I can't wait to put it onto my $8,000 Hyundai.''

NEWPAWT: To get theah, you go over the Verranzano Bridge and then the Pell Bridge. ''Red pants? Check. Topsidas? Check. Blue blayza? Check. Weejuns? Check. Blue Oxfid Sheuht? Check. Red tie wit green whales? Check. Tawtiss shell glasses? Check. Silva monogrammed belt buckle? Check. Colla pin? Check. School crest gold signet ring? Check. American Express Gold Cod? Check. Rezzavation at the White Hawse Tavvin? Check. Cah keys f'the Beema? Check. Okay, ready f'Newpawt. Les roll.''

NO SUH: I believe you're mistaken. ''Middle of nowheah? No suh. Roe Dyelin's the most ideelee located place in America. Wheah else can you be a shawt hop from both Boston and N'Yawk? The convenience is incredible. That's half the reason I live here. 'Cawse, I havvent been to Boston aw N'Yawk in 10 yizz but that's b'side the point.''

NO-STA: No, Sister. Mostly heard in Catholic schools. ''No-sta, I'm sahree, but you gave me faw wrong mocks on my geology quiz. Carolina and Wyoming ah not states, Jerusalem is not in Izz'rull and Oddick is not a continent. I know I'm right, and heah's the map to prove it: theah all small towns in Roe Dyelin.''

Rler on ski chairlift out west: "Great skeen this yeea, innit?"

Non-Rler: "Not bad. Where you from?"

Rler: "Roe Dyelin."

Non-Rler: "Sure. I have some friends who live there - near New York. They take the commuter train into Manhattan."

Rler: "That's not Roe Dyelin."

Non-Rler: "You're not that island off New York?"

Rler: "Roe Dyelin's nottapotta New Yawk."

Non-Rler: "What do you mean by 'nottapotta'?"

Rler: "Just that. Weah nottapotta New Yawk. Weah in New England. You know, Conneh'ihkit, Na'amsha..."

Non-Rler: "Na'amsha? Is that a state?"

Rler: "Shoo-wa."

Non-Rler: "Shoo-wa?"

Rler: "Shoo-wa. Yaw thinking of Lawn Guylin. I live in Roe Dyelin."

Non-Rler: "Oh. So what's your island near?"

Rler: "It's not an island, it's a state."

Non-Rler: "A whole state? You sure?"

Rler: "I'm shoowa."

Non-Rler: "I guess I don't know the east coast so well. Help me get my bearings. What's Roe Dyelin near? I mean, generally?"

Rler: "New Yawk."

The Rhode Island Dictionary

NOT F'NUH'IN: Usually used at start of sentence to emphasize truth; rare anywhere but Roe Dyelihn. Rough translation: 'I may be out of line here, but...' ''Not f'nuh'in, but if I were you, I'd go to those loyiz who advvitize on TV. They settled wit the inshurnce company f'me on a slip-n-fall f'ten-grand, and all I got was a bruised fanny. Long as it's a soft-tissue aw low-a back, they gavvintee they'll d'livva.''

NUMBA: RISDIC officials were not very skilled at adding these up. ''Thank goodness 30-yeea mawcgidge rates ah at 7 percent. I need one faw the lo-numba plate I'm bine.''

O

ONNA: Honor. "A'cawse I pay good intrist rates to the loyiz I bah-ro money from. It's a matta 'a onna. I'm a Roe Dyelin superia cawt justice."

ONNACONNA: On account of. "I'm sahree, I'm not gonna be able to go out f'dinna f'the rest of the season onnaconna my 9-yea-old's in a youth hockey league, which as you know is not a spawt in Roe Dyelin, it's a religion."

ONNIS'T'GOD: I'm not kidding. "The guhvunah was theah, the may-a of Prahvdince was theah, even the Biship was theah. All f'the openin' of a new bus shelta. Onnis't'God. And I thought they weuh gonna get into a fight ova who got t'cut the ribbon faw the camrizz. If that's not Roe Dyelin, I dunno what it is."

OSCAR: Inquire of her. "I think that's one of those restrinz wit mob connections, but I can't say f'shoowa. Let's call Ahlene on the radio and oscar. She'll know. I mean, she's the one who made the list in the feuhst place."

OTCH: Mocks stot of Atwells Avenue. "My brotha says that thing hangin' from the otch at the stot of Fedril Hill is a pine cone. I tole him - 'Waddaya, nuts? It's a pignoli.' Then Vinnie says to me, 'A pignoli? Y'both nuts. It's a pigna.' But Tony, he says weah all nuts - he lives on Atwells and he knows faw a fact it's a pineapple. Only Angela says, 'A pineapple? F'get about it.' She says we doan know nuthin'. What it really is, she says, is an aycawn. Which settles it until Vinnie's Grandma - Grandma Thereser - she says 'It's a pinea.' Which I nevva heahd of. So you know what I say? I say I dunno what it is."

OTT FE'A: Held annually in Wikfit. "I can't d'side between the matadaws on black velvet aw this flahral still-life with pink sea-shells. Maybe I'll just compromise and get this oil of seagulls wheelin' ova the ocean sunset. No wait, theah's anotha oil of seagulls wheelin' ova the ocean sunset faw fidolla cheapa. Hold on, theah's anotha one ova theah. Wait - theah's a few maw..."

OUTTASTAYTA: Anyone who's lived in Roe Dyelin less than 75 years. "I could tell he was an outtastayta when he began giving me directions by street names instead of landmocks. I stopped and said - f'get 'South on Elmgrove, right on Angell.' Around heah, we say, 'Head south passed the Dunkin' Donitz, left just afta that big Bee holding the gun at the Navy Base, and then right at the roat-ree they got rid of ten yizz ago..."

OWWA: Average wait at Twin Oaks. At 3 p.m. on a Tuesday. "We in the Genrassemblee will yoo-zhlee spend a few mih'its debay'in Creh'it Union bills, a few maw mih'its debay'in the annual budget, and maybe 10 aw 15 mih'its debay'in campaign refawm. But evvy day, we give at least an owwa to debay'in who gets which pocking spaces outside the State House. We have ah priorities straight."

OZ: Ours. "Isn't that the greatest raised backyod pool you've evva seen? And it's all oz - paid faw. Extruded aluminum deck and evvything. We only live a mile from the ocean, but me and Robbit have been dreamin' of ah own pool f'yizz. All Roe Dyelandas do."

P

P'TUCKET: Home of the world's biggest rotary: the dreaded downtown circulata. "The easiest way to spot an outlanda is to write down th'name 'Pawtucket' and see how they pvonounce it. If they say 'Pawwtucket,' theah not a real Roe Dyelinda - even if they weuh bawn heah. The true pvnunciation is 'P'tucket.' A'cawse, the rest of the country is convinced it's called 'Pawwtucket' because whenevva it makes nashnil news of any kind, 100 peuhcent - not 99 but 100 - of all outtastate TV and radio announsiz say 'Pawwtucket.' On the otha hand, I'm sure all the guys at Camp McKean in Pennsylvania - the fedril prison weah May-a You-Know-Who went - by now knows how to pvnounce it peuhfickly.''

P.S.D.S.: Pierced ears. Must be pronounced rapidly. "C'mon, ma. Evvyone else at Moses Brown has 'em. Even Jennifa came in today, and, like, she goes, 'My mom let me get P.S.D.S. yesstay. Check 'em out.' And like, heuh pearints ah membas of the Agawarm Hunt. And heuh dad's, like, cheeamin of the Univeuhsity Club's House Committee - and he letter. If you don't let me, I'll totelee, totelee die.''

PACKIE: Liquor store. Derived from 'package store.' "Gotta make a packie run to stock up faw a potty. Why? I'm commemaraytin' a mayja event in my life: I just went down to the Veekil Rej-stree faw a new license and was in an' outta theah in twenny-faw minutes - I timed it. If that's not a reason to cellbrate in Roe Dyelin, I dunno what is.''

PAHLLA: Foy-a. "Like all Roe Dyelindas, we yoosta have a Flahrider room in ah house. You know - a big pahlla. But afta a'while we d'sided why not have the real thing. So, like all Roe Dyelindas also do soona aw layta, we moved t'Flahrider itself.''

PAHSTER: Made fresh on The Hill. "Basically, if y'gonna make pahster, y'gotta know pahster. Vermicelli's like an angel's haia. Then you got the pahster cousins: spaghetti, spaghettini, bucatini and tagliatelle. Y'also got fusilli, which is like spaghetti that stuck its finga in an outlet. Rigatoni's like a tube wit ridges, though not as bigga

tube as cannelloni aw manicotti. Conchiglie's like a lodge shell and lumache's a smalla shell. Most people confuse fiochetti wit farfalle, but the feuhst is bows and the seh'in is buttaflies. Then y'got fusilli, which is cawk screws and tortiglioni which is spirals. A'cawse, rotini's spirals, too. Orzo's like rice, tubettini's like tiny macrony. And when y'think cappelletti, y'gotta think small hats. Finelee, y'got wheels. The Italian weuhd f'wheels, I think, is 'wheels.' Is that cleah? Okay, let's cook.''

PAI'IHN: What ott students study at RISD. ''I began pai'ihn my boat faw th'summa this week. My brothin-lawr stotted pai'ihn his own boat. So did my pottna rat the feuhm, my denniss, my butcha, my fommacist, my loy-a, my cah deala, my computa repeeamin, my reelata, my bah tendah and tree of my naybiz. Bottom line: evvyone in Roe Dyelin owns a boat. And evvy one 'a us spends fah maw time pai'ihn the things than sailin' 'em.''

Thelma Davis-Goin was reared in a Rhode Island accent but moved to Michigan for a few years. Not long after arriving, she went into a local department store called the J.L. Hudson company and asked for a pattern. Only she pronounced it in true Rhode Island fashion, like the World War II general's name: Patton.

The saleswoman at first looked confused, then appeared as if she understood. She told Thelma if she wanted patent leather shoes, she should go to the shoe department.

"No," said Thelma. "I want a patton." She emphasized the word more crisply this time.

Again, the saleswoman was confused. But a moment later, she seemed to figure it out.

"I'm sorry," she said, "we don't deal with patents here. You'll have to go to the Federal Building on Fort Street..."

PATTON: Pronounced like the World War II general: The marking on fabric aw wallpaper. ''I moved back home to Roe Dyelin two yizzs ago, and awready, they've locked up one legislata, two judges, tree may-iz, six loyiz, and eight creh'it union prezdints. Is it my 'magination aw is a patton fawmin' heah?''

PAW: Opposite of rich. ''People think Bruce Sundalin's rich but afta tree aw faw runs faw govuhnuh, he's now paw, mostly because of his fundraisiz. Why would a fundraiza make him paw? He holds them at his auto-tella.''

PAWDOGS: Main food group at McCoy stadium, fahllid closely by that cotton candy they sell vacuum-sealed in aluminum foil packs. ''I'll take a Pawdog at McCoy any day ovva a Portahouse Steak; and I doan even keea that Pawdogs ah on the EPA Supafund list.''

PAYPA: What this is printed on. ''Roe Dyelin definitely gets no respect around the country. Whenevva weah mentioned in an outtastate paypa, it's awliss the same kind of seh'ince: 'Texas is so big you could fit 216 Roe Dyelins inside it. Alasker is so lodge you could fit 470 Roe

Dyelins innit. I even read one that said you could fit five and a half Roe Dyelins in Hawaii. I'm sicka it. Ah we a state aw a standit of geographical meszhamint?''

PEPPIZ: Ingredient of grindas. ''I don't care what it is - a sangwidge, a pahster dish, a grinda, even breh'fiss - if you make it wittout peppiz, it's not orthentic, bona fide, unequivical, indisputable, onnis't'God Roe Dyelin. And if it is a sangwidge, and you do make it wit peppiz, but don't sell it at a Dyena aw Sub Shop, it's still not Roe Dyelin.''

PEUHFICK: The Fields Point Sewage Treatment plant's rekkit for overflowing on rainy days. ''We may well be the most covvupt state in the nation, but theah's one thing in Roe Dyelin that's definitely peuhfick. I mean tote-lee peuhfick. I mean, f'get about it it's so peuhfick. Doug White's haia.''

Julie Kliever offers a classic Rhode Island conversation she once witnessed between a native and an out-of-stater. To stress that our dialect is so distinct we even perplex close neighbors, Julie notes that the out-of-stater was a Bostonian.

"You're a good ahtist," the Rhode Islander said. "Could you drawr me a pitcha of a pore?"

"A pore?" said the Bostonian. "I don't get it. Why a pore?"

"You know. A pore. Like an animal's pore."

Now the Bostonian was even more confused. "Huh?"

"A pore," said the Rhode Islander, exasperated. "Like the bottom of a cat's foot."

She got her drawing.

PHYSICAL: Fiscal. ''I heah IBM and Genra Mottiz got into a biddin waw to hiya him as chief physical offissa. They thought he had the ideal experience to help witta teuhnaround. He's spent the last two yizzs running a reopened Rhode Island creh'it union.''

PLEECE: Officer of the law. ''I'm on the Blah Kyelin pleece fawce right now, but my real dream is to move up to a mayja-league fawce like Lih'il Compton.''

PLEECE?: Pardon me, I didn't quite get that? ''Paypa a'plastic, ma'm? Pleece? No - sahree. We don't have van'tee bags heah at Stop and Shop.''

PLEESTA?: Excuse me, Sister, I didn't hear you. ''Pleesta? No, I promise we dih'int. Me and Chevul did not hitch up ah skeuhts when the guys from St. Rafe's walked by. Well, maybe a lih'il, but only an inch.''

POCKER: Winter coat. Classic local example of moving an 'R' from wheah it belongs to wheah it doesn't. ''Don't you deah put my pocker downcella f'the summa. It's only May. If theah's a freak snowfall, I wanna be ready. Hang it heah by the flashlight, batreece, and grozeree coupons f'bread and milk''

POINT JUDE: Point Judith. "Frennamine who's a state senta tole me to meet him at Point Jude at 1 p.m. to go out onniz boat. I wait all aftanoon and he fine-lee shows up at 7 p.m. - and doesn't even apologize. I tell him, 'Y'late.' He says, 'I'm right on time.' I tell 'em, 'Senta, you said to meet at 1 p.m., but you show up at 7. That's six owwas late.' He says, 'Accawdin' to Roe Dyelin legislative time, that's downright punctual.' "

POKKABOOK: Purse. "I don't know what this weuhld is comin' to when you can't walk down the street wittout havin' someone grab y'pockkabook. It happened right on Pock Avenue. Podden me? In N'Yawk? No, Cvann-stin. Y'tellin me theah's a Pock Avenue in N'Yawk also? I nevva knew theah weuh 'two."

POME: Veuhse that rhymes. "He's one of the brightest litrittcha students in all 'a Pon-ergansett High. Listen to this love rhyme he wrote: 'From Fawsta to Glawsta I roam. That's what makes this a pome. In winna we have but one coat. We'll weah it, you and me boat."

POKKABOOK

POTS AND LAYBA: What makes an oil change cost $231. "Anotha thing weea se-cretly proud of heah in Roe Dyelin is we have one of the highest nashnil cah theft rates. Down deep, Roe Dyelindas like any-thing that makes us feuhst, even if it's un-sayvree. Evvybody has theah own reasons f'stealin' cahs. Some people do it so they can cannibalize them and avoid pane pots and layba. But most do it to make a dolla. A'cawse, these people ont exacklee Road Skahlizz. The typical Roe Dyelin cah thief steals a $20,000 Jeep Cheahkee and fences it faw $600. The only people I know who are dumba about money than that is the management of IBM, Seeas and Genril Mo-tizz. Oh yeah, and RISDIC."

WIT' POTS 'N' LAYBA THAT COMES TO ZACKLY A HUNNIT AN' FIFTEEN DOLLIS.

POTTY: What Roe Dyelin Republican Genrassemblee cannaditz never have on election night. "It says heah you held yeuh cannaditz feuhst fundraisin' potty at the Capitol Grille. I'm sahree, but by statute we at the Bawd of Eleckshins haffta reject his application f'canditzy. No one can be consih'id a legal cannadit in Roe Dyelin until you've held a fundraiza rat the 1025. Says it right heah in the Genra Lawrs."

POWWA: Membas of the Genrasemblee feel this makes their low salary weahth it. "My dream is to be Speaka. He's even got maw powwa than a radio talk show host."

PRAHVDINCE: Considdit a treszhid secret by locals; gets no respect nationally. "I'm so proud. The May-a juss gave me and my nayba Sadie, who's 92, a special city awawd f'being the last two proppity ownas in Prahvdince who still pay taxes. Evvything else in the city's a non-profit."

PREPPED OUT: Style of dress found principlee on Prahvdince's Easside. "The prepped out guys ah my favrit - especially Bif, Trip, Chip and Tad. Akchili, my favrit of all is Skip - he's so cool he's got his initials monogrammed on evvything: his belt buckle, wallet, cuff links, key chain, school ring, polo sheuht, hankachief, glasses case and some real big ones on the cuffs of his Shetland sweata so you can see them when he walks around wittit ova his shouldiz wit the ahms tied around his neck. And, like, this is so cool - he tole me this week he plans to go to Hill-house to get maw monograms put on the adhesive tape he uses to hold his Topsidas togetha."

PRIZZNIZZ: Final careah stage for 20 peuhcent of Roe Dyelin may-iz, creh'it union officials and judges. "Y'heah they had to let out a theuhd of the prizznizz from ACI Maximum on eauhly release? Had to make room f'the entiya city administrations from P'tucket and Cvann-stin. Meanwhile, that lousy Prime Time Live did a special calling us the most covvupt state in the nation. The neuhve."

PRIZZNIZZ

Q

QUESTIONNEAH: Questionnaire. "If you want to pass the bah exam questionneah, you'd betta ansa 'no' to the question about whetha loyiz in Roe Dyelin evva have any right to criticize the judishee-eahree. Oh, and make sheuh you pay y'two-hunnit dolla bah exam fee in unmocked bills."

QUOTER: Quota. "You don't seem to undastand, theah's no quoter on the amount of tuxedos I can rent at taxpaya's expense. I'm a Roe Dyelin' Spreem Cawt Justice."

R

RAHJA: First name of Rhode Island's founda. "So Rahja Williams gets kicked out of Massachusiss faw havving the same traits the rest of us moddin-day Roe Dyelindas have: not being able to get along wit anyone besides eachotha. Then he comes up Nearrgansett Bay, scoops some shellfish out of the warta, d'sides this is the spot, and suddenly runs into some Indians. 'I like y'clams,' Rahja says to them. And they say: 'The Indian weuhd faw clam is ko-hog, and if y'gonna stick around, you best not f'get it.' The rest is histree."

RALLY: Rarely. "I'm worried. I've begun to pvnounce some of my ah's as R's: I ackchili said grinder instead of grinda th'otha day. Then, last night I drove ova a half owwa just to go to a restrint. Not to mention that I now stop at yella lights and drink regula milk instead of cawfee. And I rally, rally call talk shows anymaw to express my pointa view. I'm tellin ya, if I don't straighten up, I could lose my Roe Dyelin citizenship."

RAWL: We are all. "Wanna come with us Vinnie? We've lined up the all-time most excellent possible Roe Dyelin teenage day: Feuhst, rawl goin' shoppin at the Mall, wit maybe a break f'Del's; then weah havin' lunch eitha rat the Creamree, aw New Yawk System; afta that weah hittin Skahbruh beach, aw maybe Miskwamerkit; f'dinna, we'll check out Dominoes, maybe awda a lodge wit evvything onnit; and fine-lee we go ova to Rocky Point f'the night. Waddaya say?"

RED LOBSTA: Outtastate franchise giving Rocky Point clamcakes a run f'theah money. "My favrit restrint? It used to be the Bonanzer Steak House, but then I figya'd, 'Look - I live in Roe Dyelin. By the shaw. We have a mayja fishin' innstree heah. I should eat local seafood prepeea'd the local way.' So now I go to Red Lobsta."

REE'LA'TA: Local profession which spent the 1980s selling houses in Roe Dyelin and is spending the 1990s not selling houses in Roe Dyelin. "Rememba the 80s? When you could flip the same patch of wetlans between figh condo developiz in figh munts and nevva had to worry about financin' because the same creh'it union underwrote evvy deal? Being a Roe Dyelin ree'la'ta hasn't been the same since."

REEDA: Second-grade book. "Today, children, we'll pick up in ah reeda wheah we left off in The Founding of Roe Dyelin: 'Upon establishing Roe Dyelin in the name of religious libbatee, Rahja Williams went on to establish otha local institutions. Feuhst, he drew seer-up from a local bean-like plant hovvisted by the Indians, mixed it into a pail of milk and established cawfee milk. Then he squeezed lemon from a tree into a cup of snow and established lemonade slush. Afta that, he rowed by canoe to Wawwick, wheah he established Twin Oaks and immediately found his potty-of-one would have a two owwa wait faw a table...''

REGLA: Unusual Roe Dyelin version of coffee. "I gotta tell you what I sawr today at Dunkin Donitz. This outtastayta sits down, awdas regla cawfee, and a'cawse, the waitress puts in cream and sheuga. He says, 'No - I awdid regla.' She says, 'I gave you regla.' He fine-lee explains that in most of the country, 'regla' means not decaffeinated. The waitress says, 'Not heah. Heah it means cream and sheuga.' I mean, what's with outtastaytas?''

REKKIT: What most Rhode Island politicians either have now or will soon. 'My 'ponent asks my qualifications f'the great orfuss of may-a. Feuhst and fawmost, I have no crimnul rekkit. Now that I think about it, that's my main qualification. In Roe Dyelin, it's a pretty good one.' ''

ROE DYELIN: Described by Wall Street Journal as smudge on the fast lane to Cape Card. "So get this. My new bride was bawn and raised in Manhattan. It's so big theah, heuh whole life, she's nevva seen a politician in peuhson. No guhvanah, no senta, no congreesman. Nevva even seen a city councilman aw soowa commissiona. But heuh feuhst day in Roe Dyelin, I take heuh to the Univeuhsity Club on the Easside. I want to show heuh the squash cawts, which you can only get to by walking through the men's lockaroom. That's routine - we just shout out - 'Woman coming through.' So I shout it out and we begin to walk through. Suddenly, a guy walks out of the showwa witta towel on. So I say to my new wife - 'Honey, I'd like you to meet a frennamine: Senta John Chafee.' Aftaweuhd, she says she can't bleeve it, afta nevva even mee'ihn a dog catcha in Manhattan, on heuh feuhst day heah, she meets a half-naked U.S. senta. So I tole heuh, 'Honey, get yoosta'it. That's Roe Dyelin.' ''

ROLACOASTA: Sawce of indigestion at Rocky Point Pock. "Take my advice, nevva eat a Shaw Dinna and two doughboys befaw ridin' the cawkscrew rolacoasta rat Rocky Point. Not to mention the usual tree weeniz, some cotton candy, a chawclit covvid doughnut, two clamcakes, a load a' stuffies...why y'lookin' so shocked? Roe Dyelindas nevva go to Rocky Point just t'ride. We go theah to eat.''

ROLD: Are old. Always pot of lodgea sentence. "It's ah feuhst date, I beealy know the geuhl, so I haxed her, 'Ha rold ah ya?' She said, 'That's not a polite question to hax a lady.' Then, ameejitlee, she says, 'Didju know single women outnumba single men in Roe Dyelin?' Befaw I can ansa, she says, 'Would you like to have children wit me?' This is even befaw the appetiza. My advice: nevva date a woman whose bye-logical clock you can heah ticking.''

The Rhode Island Dictionary

S

S'MENT: Typical usage: 'The only thing densa than the cash in May-a Sarault's pockets was the s'ment between his ears.' ''If Lizzie Bawdin was smot, she'd've bear-reed heuh pear-rints in s'ment neks to Jimmy Hoffer. They'd have nevva found anything. That is, unless the s'ment was used as paht of an overpass on Route 95, at which point it would have a'ventchalee caved in.''

SADDY: First day of the weekend. ''Feuhst we make a stop at Benny's. Then we head ova to Apex and Ann in Opes. Afta that we stop at Dunkin' Donitz and then go to Home Depot. We spend an owwa theah and on ah way home, stop by a few yod sales. Fine-lee, we hit Twin Oaks early to beat the crowds. Don't you just love an adult Saddy in Roe Dyelin?''

SALIT: Most locals prefer seeza. ''I'm sa-hree ma'm, you'll haffta take this back to the kitchen - I dih'int awda it. You must be new at waitressing in Roe Dyelin. When I tole you I wanted vinega, that meant I was awda'in French fries, not salit.''

S'MENT

Rler: "If you hax me, it's cleah who the greatest f'ball playa of all time was."

Non-Rler: "Who?"

Rler: "Bott Stah."

Non-Rler: "Never heard of him."

Rler: "C'mon. Everyone knows who Bott Stah is." *(Continued)*

Non-Rler: "Sorry, I've never heard of any Bott Stah. Which means most people probably haven't because I'm a football junkie."

Rler: "Well I'm glad we're eatin' inna dinah because everyone inna dinah knows spawts. Les hax the guys ova theah in the feuhst boot."

Non-Rler: "Boot?"

Rler: "Boot."

Non-Rler: "What do you mean, 'boot'."

Rler: "Boot. Where you sit."

Non-Rler: "Oh, booth."

Rler: "That's what I said. Boot. Excuse me guys. You follow football?"

Non-Rlers in booth: "Of course. We're sports junkies."

Rler: "Great. Will you tell my friend here who Bott Stah is?"

Non-Rlers in booth: "Bott Stah? Never heard of him."

SANGWIDGE: When you're not in the mood for a whole grinda. "I'm sahree, but you dih'int pass the most impaw'int pot of the DPW roadwork test, so we won't be able to hiya you. You did fine operatin' heavy equipment, you did peuhfick positioning Jeuhsey Barrias, and you were the best jack-hamma operayta I've seen all munt. But you flunked the key skill: you failed to prove you could eat a pinnabuh'ihn'jeli sandgwidge on the side the road from 10 a.m. until 2."

SCO: Let's go. "Jeet? No? Jwanna? Sco."

SCONE'ON?: What's going on? "Scone'on? Nuttin? Me neitha. Avvagood-won."

SEAV-UP: Syrup. "Wuss wrong witcha, my friend? This is not a good way to make an impression on y'new employa. Y'come to an outdaw picnic sponsid by Autocrat, and ask faw a lemonade slush? Lissen to me. Autocrat makes seav-up f'cawfee milk.

THE EARL OF SANGWIDGE

Cawfee milk is the official state drink. It beat out Del's in a no-holds-bod legislative fight. No one - I repeat no one - moves up the cawprit ladda rat Autocrat who drinks Del's. Wise up.''

SEENYIZ: 'Eld'lee. ''It awliss breaks my hot to see seenyiz struggling through a day. F'example, look at that paw guy comin' onto ah RIPTA bus right now. See him? The theuhd one in line? The really skinny one with a bad shave showin' the driva his seenya citizen cod to make sure he gets a discount? Paw guy. I think I'll stand up right now and offa Senta Pell my seat.''

SEEVE-EE-S. Serious. ''Ah u seeve-ee-s? Y'gonna really mavvy an outtatowna? Someone from East Providence? That's so fah - you live in Barrington.''

SHAW DINNA HALL: Other states may have the biggest building or mountain, but they have nuthin' on us: we have the

world's biggest Shaw Dinna Hall. It may also be the only one, but it's definitely the biggest. ''Weah especially proud of the Shaw Dinna Hall's daytime seuhviss heah rat Rocky Point. We gave the menu a lot of thought, and stressed variety. You can eitha choose clamcakes, clamcakes, clamcakes aw clamcakes.''

SHAW DINNA: State's most notable natural resawce. ''Nuthin like a full, evvything-included shaw dinna. Y'get clamcakes and chowda. Y'get a bowl of steamas and baked fish wit creole source. Y'get cawn on the cob and French fries. And weah only geh'ihn stotted heah. Once y'done wit all that, y'move on to y'half boiled chicken aw a one pound boiled Maine lobsta. 'Cawse, don't ask me why they seuhve Maine lobstas instead of Roe Dyelin lobstas - must be the old Roe Dyelin infeeree-awtee complex, but that's anotha discussion. Back to shaw dinnas: if y'in the mood, you can get a twin lobsta, linguine wit clam source, aw fish & chips. Then y'wash it all down wit wartamelon aw Indian puddin.' When y'done, if y'still hungry, theah's plenny a' doughboys around Rocky Point Pock. Oh - did I f'get to mention the co-slaw?''

SHAW: Where Rho Dyelindas dream of owning a seh'ihn home. ''People hax me why I live in Roe Dyelin. That's easy. The shaw. The ocean shaw. No state has maw ocean to its size than Roe Dyelin. They even call us the Ocean State. I love livin' by the ocean. It's what makes we Roe Dyelindas what we ah. A'cawse, I do all my swimmin' at Olney Pond since it's just down the road. Matta a'fack, I havvent been to the ocean in ten yizz. Make that 15 yizzs. But it's theah. Which is why I love livin' in Roe Dyelin."

SHAYVA: The cawdless, rechodgeable is prefeuhed model. "I'm goin' on Ahlene's tawk show this aftanoon to rebut chodges that we legislatas ahnt that intelligent. Peuhsonlee, I think that's slanda. And to make sure the liss'nin audience gets a good impression of us, I'm takin' my shayva to give my face a last-minute once-ova befaw the show."

SHOCK: Often swims with fin out of water. "The lifegods just called evvyone outta the warta - sposelee someone spotted a shock. But peuhsonlee, me and my friend Chevul ah maw conseuhned about the shocks on the beach. You know, the male ones with neckchains. I mean, this is Skahbruh afta all."

SHOOTIZ: Restaurant known for displaying meat. "My husband Larry thinks he's some piece a' weahk, so he was thrilled when the ownas of Shootiz gave in to all the politically correct pressha and agreed to add a seh'in hot bod contest to featcha men as well as women. I kept tellin' him, Larry, yeuh not 25 anymaw, yeuh 45 - and y'look like a typical 45-yeea-old Roe Dyelin male. But he was convinced he'd win so he went to sign up. Paw guy, they wou'int even let him enta. They tole him he'd have a betta shot as Pizza Hut Man-of-the-Yeea. Aw maybe the Dunkin' Donitz Posta Boy. He dih'int think that was vear-ee funny."

SHOOWA: Sure. "Shoowa - I'd love to join you and the geuhls f'some shoppin at Goddin City t'mahrra. Saddy is Andy's day to play Bocce anyway. 'Cawse, Sundy is his day to play golf. Mondy's his night to play cods. Tuesdee's his tennis night. Wennsdee's his night t'go to the dogs. Theuhsdee's his Democratic city committe mee'ihn. Fridee he goes to Jai Alai. Then Saddy's bocce time again. That Andy of mine shoowa is busy, innee?"

SHOPPER IMAGE: High end catalogue. "I'm awda'ing evvything. Feuhst, I want the Splash-Blasta Squeuht Rifle, then the 'lectronic golf toota and the black loafas made in Itlee. I want the Hawse Race Analyza, the Pleece Raida Detecta, the Steah Climba and fine-lee, the Digital Pulse Monita to make sure I'm not about to take a hot attack. Can't be too caffle at my age about the ole ticka. Then again, maybe I'll just toss the catalogue and go to Ann in Opes. I'm a Roe Dyelinda. My theory: if Ann in Opes doesn't havvit, I don't need it.''

SHUV-A-LAY: Make of cah. ''I just had my '83 Shuv-a-lay Camaro appraised - you know, the one I ride around downtown Prahvdince all day wit my tunes cranked up? Got the figyas right heah. Cah value: $1,250. Stereo: $3,895. Do I got my priorities right, awwutt?''

SINKA: Doughnut. ''Think I'll head down to Dunkin' Donitz, get a cawfee, and then come home and drink it nex t'my cawfee machine. Why botha goin' out? 'Cause I can't drink my mawnin' cawfee wittout a sinka t'go wittit. Why not make my own cawfee? Dumb question. Roe Dyelindas awliss drink Dunkin Donitz cawfee neks to theah own cawfee machine. Don't you know anything?''

SIZZIZ: Cutting instruments. ''Take it from one who's been theah: If yeuh gonna survive emotionally as a state legislata, the feuhst thing you haffta buy is a sizziz. Then you tell y'seckaterry to get the Jeuhnal-Bulletin befaw you see it, and cut out anything written about you. Anything. Ah rekkits show the Jeuhnal hasn't written a single nice ahticle about a Roe Dyelin legislata since 1963, and even that time, they prinn'id a covvection the neks day sane they musta made a mistake.''

SKAHBRUH: A favorite Roe Dyelin beach; must have big hair or be named Vinnie to be admitted. ''I'm 'fraid Dahris is a Ko-hog shy of a bushel these days. She says some men from Mahz came down to heuh backyahd outta a' fline sawsa, grabbed heuh son Vinnie and gave him six owwas of med'cul tests to figya out the sawce of some strange light signals comin' outta South County durrin' the summa months. Sposely, when Vinnie fine-lee haxed why him, they said because he's a lifegod from the epicenta of the signals. So he said, 'Oh, shoo-wa - you mean Skahbruh? It's the sun's glare off the neckchains on the men.' ''

SLANDA: Characta assassination. If you've nevva been the tahget of this, you've nevva run for orfuss in Roe Dyelin. ''My opponent accuses me of being anti-Italian, but that's slanda. You want proof? I eat suppa rat Angelo's all the time. I love the gvayvy.''

SMATTTA WITCHA: What seems to be the difficulty? ''Why doncha evva lissen to me, Hahvey? I tole ya theah was a stawm wawnin, but you ignawwed me. Now weah out on the highway and y'whypizz don't weahk, even though I tole you to get them fixed lass munt. And we should nevva have gone to that movie anyway, because you know I hate ones that ah rated 'ah.' And you know the last thing I like to do is nag my uhzbin, but this is ah anniveuhsree, and the least you could've done was taken me inna lemmazeen to my favrit restrint, the Ahlive Goddin, instead of out faw frozen yohggit and a bad movie. And look at this traffic - when it vains in Roe Dyelin, its the loruv'th'jungle on the highways. And y'making me miss my favrit TV show Hod Koppy. Hahvey - c'nigh hax you a question? Smattta witcha?''

SODER: Soft drink. "We have so many dropped 'ahz' in this state, we had to put them somewheah. So instead of sane 'soda,' evvyone heah uses the weuhd 'soder' azza home f'the ahz."

SOOPA: Outstanding. "You can awliss tell how soopa a Roe Dyelin hot dog is by how long you can taste it aftaweuhd. New Yawk System is definitely soopa - you can taste those the neks mawning. Then theah's Saugys - you can taste those through the weekend. But I don't think anything is as soopa as Haven Brothas - those stay wit you a whole season."

SOOPAMAN: The comic hero who did not leap the old Industrial National Bank building in the show's intro footage after all. "The guy breaks his neck in two places in a cah axxident, then comes back and stots winnin' weuhld class boxing matches within six months. I'm tellin' ya, if The Paz isn't Soopaman, nobody is."

SORIT: Having glimpsed something. "I cou'int bleeve they weuh sellin' it right theah in the counta in that Fox Point fish mocket. I sorit wit my own eyes. When I haxed what it was, the man said it depends. He calls it octopus, the new Yuppies call it calamari and the old guys from the naybahood call it bait."

SOURCE: Sauce. "Trust me, y'can't seuhve a Dynamite wit only hambeuhg, mushrooms, cehree, unyinz, chili powda and peppiz. What makes a Dynamite is the source. T'mayta source, mixed wit t'mayta puree, pawwed into a long - I mean long - tawpeeda roll. Expeuhts give the source a kick wit some crushed red peppa. Plus you can't just seuhve a dynamite at a nawmul potty; it's gotta be a beeya and dynamite potty wheah you raise money faw chairtee. How do I know? I grew up in Winsocket, that's how. Any questions?"

SOW COUNTY: Consists of evvything south of that Towwa on Route 1. For those who live theah, anything nawta the towwa is kinsiddid anotha weuhld. "My sista? She lives way down Sow County. Technically, she's only 10 miles from me in Wawwick, but theahs no such thing as simply 'Sow County' in Roe Dyelin. It's awliss, 'Way down' Sow County.'"

SOW KINGSTON: Home of You-Ah-Eye. "Weea still proud of havin' made Roe Dyelin famous faw a week. Rememba when Prezdint Reagan said unemployment wasn't a real issue since nobody really keea'd when someone in Sow Succotash got laid off? It teuhns out the only place in America called Succotash is in Sow Kingston and reportas from all ova came down to get quotes. Only no one from Succatash would give them quotes because theah all a bunch of Roe Dyelin Swamp Yankees and don't bleeve in makin' a fuss about nonsense."

SOWWA BAWLS: Popula hod candy. "You nevva heuhd of sowwa bawls? Neks to pizzer, it's the mayja food group f'kids at Cvann-stin East."

SPIVVIT: Spirit. "Feuhst the Wall Street Jeuhnal calls us a 'Smudge on the fast lane to Cape Card;' then Prime Time Lives calls us the most covvupt state in the nation. But y'can't kill Roe Dylandas spivvit. Deep down, we ahselves know weea nobla than that - that's what my uncle the state senta says, who got me my job wit DOT."

SQUEET: A word that comes from saying the following phrase at lightning speed: Let's go eat. "Jeet? No? Squeet."

STAHCASE: Local movie theater with 347 screens and 'small' popcorns that could feed livestock. "Waddaya say we check out the Stahcase Cinemer - I heah 'Terminata's' playin'. Aftaweuhd, we can check out the lobby ott gal-ree. I heuhd it won an awawd f'being the greatest collection of bad ott unda a single roof in the country."

STAHRIDGE: Where Roe Dyelindas place emergency items downcella. "Best fridge-rayta I evva had: comes wit ice dispensa, tree - count 'em tree - stahridge draws, and a soopa-lodge freeza that can hold a munt's supply of bread and batreece in case of snow."

STATIE: State Troopa. Force made Roe Dyelin proud to this day by being named nation's best dressed. "In 20 yizzs, I nevva once arrested any big time cons, but I still made the Statie Hall of Fame faw goin onta Davit Lettamin to model ah unifawm."

STEEMIZ: Clams. "It's easy. Lih'il neks ah small clams you eat cold. Steemiz ah big clams you eat hot. And ko-hogs ah bigga clams you make chowda outta. Got it?"

Rler: "Jeet?"

Non-Rler: "Pardon?"

Rler: "Jeet?"

Non-Rler: "What do you mean by 'jeet'?"

Rler: "I mean y'unngry? Y'ad suppa yet? Jeet?"

Non-Rler: "Jeet?"

Rler: "I'll say it slowa. Joozeet?"

Non-Rler: "What does 'joozeet' mean?"

Rler: "It means 'joozeet?'"

Non-Rler: "Again, please?"

Rler: "Have you eaten yet?"

Non-Rler: "Oh. I'm sorry. No. Thanks for asking."

Rler: "Squeet."

Non-Rler: "Squeet?"

Rler: "Yes. You said you haven't eaten. Squeet."

Non-Rler: "I'm not sure I follow you. Slower please."

Rler: "You know - squeet. Say 'let's go eat' real fast and it comes out as 'squeet.' At least in Roe Dyelin it does."

Non-Rler: "Oh. Gotcha. Fine. Let's go eat."

Rler: "Wutchin the mood faw? A grinda aw gaggiz?"

Non-Rler: "Pardon?"

Rler: "A teuhkey sangwidge aw weeniz?"

Non-Rler: "I'm still not sure I follow."

Rler: "A sangwidge aw hot dogs?" *(Continued)*

STOOPIT: Not a Road skahlla. "I'm not stoopit. Azza creh'it union executive, I would nevva betray the depositiz by racing to witdraw my own money afta hearing privately that the state was about to close us down. So I'll say it one maw time: that hunnit thousin dollis I took out was not a witdrawal - it was a transaction."

STUFFIES: More clams. "Where was I? I awready tole you about lih'il neks, steemiz and ko-hogs. Then theah's stuffies. Those ah ko-hogs you d'side to stuff instead of making chowda outta. Cleah?"

SUFFIX: Night lawr school in Boston - neccessary stop for Roe Dylandas on way to the state bah. "Waddaya mean wheah am I apline? Suffix nights. Only lawr school in the country witta my-na in TV advitizin f'loyiz."

Non-Rler: "Oh. Nothing that heavy I think."

Rler: "I guess I agvee. It's twirly tweet."

Non-Rler: "Twirly tweet?"

Rler: "Too early to eat. Jwanna cawfee instead?"

Non-Rler: "Pardon?"

Rler: "Juss what I said. Jwanna cawfee?"

Non-Rler: "Oh - do I want to have a cup of coffee? Sure."

Rler: "Great. So we unnastand eachotha. While weah on the way, les pick up the Sundee Paypiz."

Non-Rler: "Uh, what are paypiz?"

Rler: "Nevvamind. Les juss sco."

Non-Rler: "Sco? Could you repeat that please?"

SUH'IM: Something. "Lemee tell ya suh'im - f'the last time. I don't live in East Prahvdince. I live in Rumfit. And my boyfriend doesn't live in East Prahvdince eitha - he lives in Rivvaside. In fact, nobody lives in East Prahvdince - theah all in eitha Rumfit aw Rivvaside. F'ya don't bleeve me, hax 'em."

SUMMA: Used by most of Roe Dyelin azza verb. "My grandmotha summa'd in Oaklin Beach, but now we summa in Bonnit Shaws. I'm hoping my kids will summa in Newpawt, and my grand-kids will fine-lee make it to real paradise by summa'ing at the Dunes Club."

SUMMASET: Somerset. "She weahks in Roe Dyelin, shops in Roe Dyelin, socializes in Roe Dyelin, reads Roe Dyelin newspapiz and watches Roe Dyelin TV - she ack-chili thinks she's a Roe Dyelinda. But I had to explain, 'Brender, I'm sahree. You live in Summaset. That's ova the line. You may as well live in Rangoon.' That upset heuh so much she asked if I would at least consida heuh a borda-Roe Dyelina. I said, okay, okay - if it's so impaw'int to you, you're a borda-Roe Dyelinda. That is, afta all, a legitimate sub-species of rezdint."

SUNDALIN: Silva-haia'd Roe Dyelin guhvunah. "Sundalin? A'cawse it az tree syllables - dint you know that? Just like eacha Ant-knee Sollmin's names have two."

The Rhode Island Dictionary

SUP?: What is going on? Common among teenagers nationally, but here in particula. Longer use: Wussup? ''Sup? Some ice cream? Great. At Big Alice's? You mean that place all the magazines say seuhves some of the best ice cream in the country? Nah. I'm a Roe Dyelin teenayja. I'd ratha just hang on the sidwalk outside the Deary Mott across the street and eat Eskimo Pies from the freeza.''

SUPPA: Late lunch. ''It's easy; Roe Dyelindas eat dinna instead of lunch and suppa instead of dinna. Got it?''

SWAMPA: Swamp Yankee. ''He's the tenth genration of his family who's lived down Perryville way in Sow County. Névva leaves. I was outta town faw a week; when I got back, I asked him if theah was any news. 'Big news,' he said. 'Tom's dog got skunked.' I said, 'Zattit?' He said, 'Well, lemme think. Oh yes - theah's otha news. The wind shifted to the east.' Then he asked me how things weuh up nawth. I began to tell him about Prahvdince, but he stopped me. 'I said up nawth,' he repeated. So I ast: 'Isn't Prahvdince up nawth?' He saiid: 'Not by my standits,', and tole me he meant Wickfit. If theah was evva a Swampa, it's him.''

Rler: "I'm going out to do my staws."

Non-Rler: "Do your what?"

Rler: "My staws."

Non-Rler: "I thought you were going shopping."

Rler: "I am. I'm doin my staws."

Non-Rler: "I don't think you have time to do both that and your shopping."

Rler: "Both?"

Non-Rler: "Do me a favor. Will you please agree to only go shopping?"

Rler: "I promise. I will only do my staws."

Non-Rler: "I think I'm not getting through."

Rler: "You ah. I promise to only do my staws. Includin' a packie-run at the end."

Non-Rler: "Now you're adding yet another errand? What's a packie-run?"

Rler: "A packie's a likka staw. Don't we need likka faw the potty?"

Non-Rler: "Likka for the potty?"

Rler: "I'll see ya layta. I'm doin' my staws."

Non-Rler: "But when will you do your shopping?"

T

T'MAHRRA: Tomorrow. ''Chesta's neuhviss. He's got t'head into the city t'mahrra. Not an easy thing faw an old Swamp Yankee from Burraville, but he's got business t'take cairve. I hope the traffick isn't too much faw'im. Pascoag can be a bustling place.''

TAH: Ashfawt. ''The crew just covvid the driveway this mawnin'. So pleece pock y'cah in the yahd til dahk so you don't mah the tah.''

TAHDDA SOURCE: Popula condiment. ''Me and Vichit awready half the weddin plan figya'd out. It'll be at the Venus, a'cawse. As fah as the menu, that was a hod choice faw awhile. Then I asked my friends Chevul, Dot and Lizabit what they seuhved and they all had the same ansa. Chicken and shells, tahdda source on the side.''

TEUHNIN' SIGNAL: Optional equipment on Rhode Island cahs. ''I got this new pipeline to sell used cahs. Instead of sellin' them off the lot heah, I hoe-sale 'em to a deala in New Jeuhsy. He loves 'em. Tells all his customiz the teuhnin' signals have nevva been touched.''

TH'ILL: Unlike 'College Hill,' this one only needs a 'The,' - or rather 'Th' - in front of it. ''You want the country's most seev-ee-us pahster, peppiz, pine nuts, pesto, pro-volone, parmigiano, ekspresso, esprit and politicians? Nada a problem. Th'ill.''

THAYA & WATAMIN: Intasection wheah Brown undergrads only cross on foot when the light is red. ''I don't keah what the light says at Thaya and Watamin, faw $24,000 a yeea in tuition, I'm gonna cross when I want.''

TIE IT: How you feel when you're ready for bed. ''I've been feeling so tie it since I got pregnant. I'm glad weah fine-lee seein'

The Rhode Island Dictionary

the obstrician t'mahrra. Me and my uhzbin? 'Cawse not. Like all Roe Dyelin women, I see the obstrician wit my motha.''

TIE'NOLLS: Non-aspirin pain relieva. Usually stated in plural with the word 'the' in front of it. ''I've been takin' the Tie'nolls faw a headache and feeva f'tree days but it's still theah. I've got the artheritis, too, and the Tie-nolls dih'int help that much eitha. Not to mention my salvation glands ah swellin' up and my flea bites is cloggin' my ahtreez in my legs again. So I called my sista who's takin' me eitha to The Miriam, The Kent aw The Roe Dyelin; probbly The Roe Dyelin since they half the best extensive care unit.''

TIVVATON: Little Compton Wannabee. ''All I wanna know is how come I can dial direct - no toll call - across state lines to Seekonk, but need to dial a '1' feuhst to call my motha-in-lawr in Tivvaton? Or my bruthin-lawr in Nawt Kingston? Wait a minute - now I read in the paypa that afta decades, they've just changed that. Great. Now we have to dial a '508' to call Seekonk even if we live only a block away ova the line. If that's not a reason to annex Seekonk as paht of Roe Dyelin, I don't know what is.''

TIYA: Cah wheel. ''Nicest Sow County nayba you'd evva want. I tole him I was drivin' into Wawwick from down heah in Tuckatown. He cou'int bleeve I was goin' all that way and back in one day. So he loaded up my pick-up wit an extra speah tiya just in case. Even gave me the name of his relltives in Wickfit 'so I can stop half-way.''

Rler riding on 95 with a non-Rler: "Wuddja use y'teuhnin' signal faw?"

Non-Rler: "Because I just switched lanes."

Rler: "Nevva use y'teuhning signal in Roe Dyelin. You'll confuse people. Hey - that guy on the Holly's trine to pass us. Don't let him in."

Non-Rler: "Holly?"

Rler: "Holly. The mottacycle."

Non-Rler: "Oh - Harley. Why not let him in?"

Rler: "Because in Roe Dyelin, it doesn't matta if you get someweah fast, as long as no one else gets theah fasta."

Non-Rler: "I see."

Rler: "Now pass th'pick-up in front a' us with the top blowin' in the breeze."

Non-Rler: "There's no top blowing in the breeze."

Rler: "A'cawse there is - that big black top."

Non-Rler: "Oh. Tarp. I can't pass him. Someone's next to him in the high speed lane."

Rler: "Who said anything about the high speed lane? That's not the passin lane in Roe Dyelin. Pass him on the right - that's the passing lane."

Non-Rler: "You sure?"

Rler: "I'm shoowa. And roll down y'winda in case you might wanna communicate with him the Roe Dyelin way."

Non-Rler: "What way would that be?"

Rler: "Nevvamine."

Non-Rler: "Nevvamine?" *(Continued)*

TOOWA: Tour. A way to get people from New Jersey who own Winnebagos to pay for the Newport mansions now that the Vanderbilts are gone. ''Welcome to the Real Roe Dyelin Toowa Bus, the one that skips the Chaymba of Commiss sights and gives you a glimpse of what weah really about. Onna left we have a group of Roe Dyelindas spendin' theah entiya aftanoon callin radio tawk shows. Onna right, we have a crowd of locals sleepin' on the sidewalk outside the Veekil Rej-stree so they can be feuhst in line to claim theah choice of van-tee license plates in the mawnin'. Onna left we have a mo'trist doin' the 'Roe Dyelin' slide through a stop sign. Onna right we have a Roe Dyelinda wit limited qualifications gettin' a state job through a relative. Onna left we have a Swamp Yankee from Fawsta in a stayta shock because he's got to drive all the way to Prahvdince and back in one day. And fine-lee, onna right we have a group of women stopping at theah cawna staw to play Keno befaw goin to the State House to protest a proposal faw a casino.''

Rler: "Right. F'getabouttit. Juss stop checkin' y'meera; we nevva do that in this state. Oh - and look what's comin' up. Slow way down."

Non-Rler: "Slow down on Route 95? Why?"

Rler: "Doncha see? Theah's an axxident on th'otha side."

Non-Rler: "So why slow down?"

Rler: "In Roe Dyelin, y'spoze-ta stop and gawk faw a few minutes."

Non-Rler: "But we'll back up traffic behind us. I've never done such a thing."

Rler: "Nevva? Gedaddaheah."

Non-Rler: "I will."

Rler: "That's not how I meant it. Look out - someone's trying to pass again; don't let him in..."

TOTE-LEE: Entirely. ''Like, I saw Mocky Mock at the Civic Senta last night and he is so tote-lee cool you wou'int bleeve it. Me and Linder had front row seats and during one paht could've touched his jockey shawts, but then we looked at eachotha and said, 'The sisstiz'll kill us on Monday at Bay View if they find out,' so we dih'int.''

TREE: Can be found in Roe Dyelin between 'two' and 'faw.' ''That's the last time I pock in that lot. I ended up wit tree dings on my daw. I buy a mint-condition Thundabeuhd - and ba-bing, ba-bing - it gets tree dings the feust week I own it. And one of them is almost as big as pin-head. So I did the only logical thing. I got the whole cah repainted.''

TREHSZHAH: The office most people still feel is held by Ant-Knee Sollmin. ''I'm def'nitely votin' faw him. Best cannadit I've seen around heah in a long time. Look at his campaign bro-shoowa: 'Vote Paul Johnson f'Trehszhah: Nevva Been Indicted.' Wit that kind of rekkit, the guy's a shoo-in.''

TRINTY: Local theater. "Why do I live in Roe Dyelin? Because it's hoddley the kind of back-wata you outta-staytas think it is. Among otha things, we have a weuhld class theata: Trinty. It's even won a Tony. It's the kind of cultural jewel that makes livin' heah special. I love Trinty. Ev-vyone does. I even went to a play theah once in the late 1980s."

TROTE: Gets saw when you have a cold. "The docta think's I have a saw trote and wants me to take pennercillen. He even gave me a p'scription, but I'm not botha'in. What do I need penercillen faw to soothe my trote? I got a Del's stand at th'end of my street."

TWIRLY: No thank you, it's too early. "My political handliz tole me it's time to stot campaignin', but I told them it's outta the question. Much twirly. The eleckshin's 22 monhts away. The Roe Dyelin public de-seuhves some relief from it all. I refuse to stot faw at least anotha week."

Rler from South Country: "You'd betta get back to y'motel befaw the snow flies."

Non-Rler: "You mean falls."

Rler: "Flies. Snow doesn't fall in Sow County. It flies."

Non-Rler: "Actually, this is my first time here. Exactly what part of Rhode Island is South County anyway?"

Rler: "Everything this side of the towwa."

Non-Rler: "The towwa?"

Rler: "The towwa. You doan wanna go nawta th'towwa unless you half to. Everything nawta the towwa is The City. Those folks ah dif'rint than we ah."

Non-Rler: "As a matter of fact, I do have to head back to the city."

Rler: "You don't have a local motel?"

Non-Rler: "I'm afraid not. I'm in a Providence hotel."

Rler: "I'm sahree."

Non-Rler: "Why are you sorry?"

Rler: "By my figya'n, that's a good theuhty miles."

Non-Rler: "So? In New York, I commute double that twice a day."

Rler: "Shoowa hope you make it befaw the snow stots fline."

Non-Rler: "Not a problem."

Rler: "I wouldn't be so shoowa. It'll take y'fevva to get theah."

Non-Rler: "Fevva? What's fevva?"

Rler: "A meszha of distance."

Non-Rler: "I see. Well, what measured distance would you classify as forever?"

Non-Rler: "Anything nawta th'towwa."

The Rhode Island Dictionary

U

UHZBIN: What Liz Taylor had eight of. "Heuh uhzbin's a Roe Dyelin politician. She pretty much stays outta the limelight except when she comes out to hold his hand during the press conferences afta his indictments."

UNDERNEET: Underneath. "Underneet, underneet. Underneet! Hand me the money underneet the desk f'God's sake."

V

V-C-AH: Used f'recawdin movies. "People don't realize how much we stand out nationally. Maybe no prezdints were bawn heah, but we've got some of the most famous people around. Let me get out my V-C-AH and prove it. Heah we go - I recawded an episode of America's Funniest Home Videos. But f'get the show itself, let's go right to the creh'its at the end. Bingo. See that frozen frame? See that name? Vin di Bona. Actual creata of America's Funniest Home Videos. Grew up in Creanston. Nevva say Roe Dyelin isn't famous."

VALENTIMES: Hearts. "It's hod to be a Roe Dyelin male on Valentimes day. In most states, all you haffta do is buy flowwiz. Heah, if you don't put a cutsey pome to y'geuhlfriend aw wife in that special section in the paypa, she's mad at you f'the neks week."

VAN'TEE PLATES. Owned by 93.4 percent of adult Roe Dyelindas, even though only 82 percent own cahs. "Tree munts ago, nobody'd evva heuhd of him; now they say he's a shoo-in faw guhvanah neks week. His platfawm is to offa free van'tee plates faw evree-one: most briwyint political promise I evva sawr around heah."

ANKA, AGAIN

OCEAN STATE
LONUMBA
RHODE ISLAND   MAY

VAN'TEE PLATE

Dan Davnfart

VICHIT: First name of forma loo-teh'it guhvanah. "Vichit Beuhtin? The acta? Liz Tayla's ex? When he was alive, he coulda put his shoes unda my bed any time."

VICTA AND RAYFA: Friends named Victor and Rafer. "Me and Victa have fawmed an exclusive Roe Dyelin club f'guys bawn wit an 'ah' at the end of theah names - but have nevva had it pvonounced. I'd like to introduce Ahtha, Alexanda, Christopha, Peeta, Fletcha, Palma, Ahcha, Cahta, Coopa, Hahpa, Baxta, Brewsta, Conna, Frayza, Cuttla, Rahja, Deava, Tucka, Whittaka, Grova, Hunta, Websta, Weuhna, Tayla and Tyla. Ak-chili, it's maw like a suppawt group than a club. It's a hod life faw us. Theah's also a women's group who have the oppsit problem. They have the letta 'a' at the end of theah names, but it awliss comes out as 'r.' I have theah membaship list right heah. Eaver, Louiser, Roader, Debbrer, Barbrer, Linder, Monicker, Virginyer, Rosanner, Laurer, Clarer, Gretter, Julier, Sarer, Marsher, Dahner, Glorier, Melisser, Lizer and Teener. At theah neks meetin', I heah theah gettin' a guest lektcha from Senta Pell's wife Nualer."

VIH-TREE: What Roe Dyelin Republicans hope to achieve in the Genrasemblee by the yeea 2020. "Once again, election day was a great vih-tree faw ah pahty in Roe Dyelin: 87 peuhcent of ah cannaditz won theah races, thus proving an old local truth: in Roe Dyelin, God is a Democrat."

VINEGA: Preferred condiment for French fries. "McDonald's headkwawtiz outside Chicago cou'int bleeve it, but we showed them the figyas and they agreed. Roe Dyelin's McDonald's franchises had the lowest peuhcentage of French fry sales in the whole weuhld. So they began puttin' vinega right on the counta neks to the ketchup in the same size sealed tin foil wrappas. Bingo - now weah sellin' as many French fries as anyone."

VISTA: Local Catholic newspaypa. "Why should livin' in Tamper, Flahrider make me feel out of touch wit Roe Dyelin? I read the Vista evvy week. No - not a subscription, my sista sends it down. Isn't that how evvyone gets the Vista in Flahrider? She sends down the Jeuhnal's Sunday magazine, too - the Roe Dyelinda. I mostly get it to see those old pitchiz in 'The Way We Weuh' featcha. I'm maw intristed in what was goin' on fawty yizzs ago in Roe Dyelin than now."

Greg Whiting works as a bartender at Shooters, and feels there are few vantage points better than that for hearing Rhode Islandese.

Of course, many customers order beeya, the favorite being Caws or Caws Light.

In summer, a Dakree is popular, especially wit strawbreeze.

Girls from Cranston, he says, prefer a drink called a Lazer Beam - pronounced Lay-za Beam.

The most popular brand of scotch - or skatch - seems to be Doowah's.

But Vokka is a popular likka too, especially mixed with tah-nik. It costs tree dollis.

Girls from Nawt Prahvdince seem partial to Kloor, used to make sombrayros.

B'cah-dee is a favorite as well, sometimes wit a lime.

Those who like a tah-keela shot seem to order Jose Cuervo, referred to simply as Kweervo.

And a well-liked tropical drink is a Rum Runna.

Then there is the mahtini crowd, which likes Beef-eetah. And the 7-and-7 crowd which likes C-grumms.

Those partial to lickrish-flavored likka like Zambooka.

Finally, wine aficionados often order that well-known brand of white wine from California, Shadnay.

Oh, and one more note. Everyone is aware that if they don't behave themselves, they'll have to deal with the bownsah.

W

WADAYATHINK'AHMIN'IDIOT'AWWUTT? I hope you realize I'm not unintelligent. ''You expect me to rent this appottment? It's fulla cocka-roaches. Wadayathink'ahmin'idiot'aw-wutt?''

WADDAYA: What are you? ''Waddaya, nuts? Y'gonna get cah inshurnce befaw y'get caught?''

WANTHIDA: Wanted to. ''I said to him, 'I wanthida ask you something. Ah these leftoviz in this Tuppaweah still good?' He said, 'I dunno, they've been theah ova a week.' I said, 'A week? F'gettit. Theah not lefotoviz anymaw; theah gottagoes.''

WARN: East Bay town. ''Barrington may have rich people, and Bristol the parade, but they got nuthin' on us because we in Warn have, um, give me a seh'in, I know theah's something big heah, it'll come to me...right: a great shoe sto-wuh.''

WARSH: What the machine downcella does to your clothing. ''Took my warsh to the same cleansas Bruce uses and they got the two of ahs mixed up. What am I s'posed to do wit ridin' britches?''

WAWWICK - Also pronounced War'rick. Contrary to what your stewardess tells you, this is wheah your plane has landed. ''The beaches ah just too fah - almost twenny minutes from ah house in Wawwick. So weah reh'in a cottage on the shaw f'the summa.''

WEELA: Private school in Providence. ''I had a straight-A average and was my gramma school's top spawts stah, but Weela wou'int admit me to its high school - neitha would any of Roe Dyelin's private schools f'that matta - because I don't meet the key entrance rekwiah-mint. My pearents don't own a Vovo station wagon.''

WES'TUHLY: Like all places 40 miles or more from Prahvdince, locals continue to doubt it's really pot of Roe Dyelin, maps notwitstanding. ''Wes'tuhly definitely has the most innerestin' beaches in Roe Dyelin. Stot wit Napatree Point - it twists halfway across the Atlantic. Then theah's Watch Hill, East Beach, and Miskwammerkit. Don't hax me how one town can have both Watch Hill, which you can only visit if yeuh a Vandabilt, and Miskwammerkit, which is

The Rhode Island Dictionary

faw the big-haia-and-gold-neckchain crowd, but they do. There's also Atlantic Beach, Dunes Pock Beach and Weekapaug. I think theah's even a piece of Kwonachaug in theah somewheah. But best of all, Wes'tuhly has its own eeapawt so you can fly theah from Wawwick.''

WHY'JA: Stot of a question. Why did you? ''Why'ja go to LaSalle, PC and Suffix in the feuhst place if you dih'int want to be a legislata?''

WICKFIT: Site of annual ott fe'a. ''It goes like this. Prahvdence was established by Rahja Williams to symbolize a place open to all faiths. Newpawt was established to eventchilly god the entrance to Neeargansett Bay from intrudiz. Fine-lee, Wickfit was established so Websta's dictionary would have a place to refeuh to unda the definition of 'Quaint.' ''

WICKIT: A Roe Dyelin teenayja's description of something impressive. Also used nationally, but pervasive here. ''Ah you seev-ee-iss? If I get a job as flag girl at a highway contruction site they'll let me weea my feuh coat? And pay me, too? Wickit. How do I apply?''

WINNA - Winner. Also, winter. ''He got the numba one winna in the drawrin' - a hunnit thousand dollis - but says theah's no way he's goin' out on this kind of winna day to colleck his winnin's.

WINSOCKET: Located side by each to Nort Smiffeel. ''He said he dih'int undastand the sign. I said, What's t'undastand? Juss read it: 'Bend y'head. Low ceiling.' He said, 'How do you bend y'head?' I tole 'em it means to bend ova. Then we walked inside, and on ah way out, I said, 'Close th'light.' He said he dih'int undastand. I said, 'What's t'undastand? Close th'light.' He juss shook his head, so I had to teuhn it off myself. Anyway, then he asks me how long I've been livin' in this house. I tole him, 'I moved heah last Motch, afta spendin' a yeea livin' on top of my uncle and anotha yeea livin' on top of my ahnt.' You wou'int bleeve the look he gave me when I said that. Guy's obviously's not from Winsocket.''

WISSTA: Worcester. ''I've heuhd of Wissta but I've nevva been theah. Too fah. I live in Winsocket.''

WITCHA: With you. ''Two-bee onnis witcha, as may-a, I cou'int possiblee accept bribes. I ab-haw bribes. Howevva, I'm sponsa'ihn a special $10,000 a plate 'time' f'myself limited to city contractiz, and I just happen to have a ticket right heah, and if you're really seev-ee-us about bid-din' f'the bridge job...''

WUJJAGIT?: What did you receive. ''Stanley, they just had the drawrin' on channel 12 and the numbas sound familia. Wujjagit again? Because if we win, we'll be able to have ah dream - the same dream Guhvanuh DiPrete had. Weah gonna buy a Winnebago and drive to Disney-weuhld, spendin' nights in McDonald's pocking lots along the way.''

WUTTA BUMMA: Expression after concert that wasn't as wickit as hoped. ''Wutta bumma, I got tickets faw Madonner at the Civic Senta, but she cancelled and they put in what they called the feuhst evva reunion of the surviving Beatles instead. Like I'm sposed to be impressed? Who ah the Beatles anyway? I nevva once sawr them on MTV. My friend tole me theah kind of like the Frank Sinatra of the baby boomers, but I thought it was a waste of a night. We should've gone to the warta-slide at Miskwammerkit instead and picked up geuhls.''

A clerk from Enterprise Hardware on Atwells Avenue offers a classic Rhode Islandese anecdote. He explained that he spends a fair amount of time fixing windows for customers. Only he has found that 99 percent of all Rhode Island customers pronounce it "winda" or "windas."

One day, he decided to test something out. He put a sign on the counter about the store's win-dow policy. The sign said: "All windas and screens must be paid in advance."

He left it there for many days. Customers came in needing repairs, read the sign without a second thought, and simply said, "How much do I owe you?"

Dozens of such customers came in. And as long as the sign was there, not a single person ques-tioned the spelling of 'windas.' "